F. B. Klynstra · Nobility of the Desert

NIJMEH (Siglawi-Rajiha).
Abbayah, foaled 1956 in Rabbah, Jordan.
Breeder: Sheikh Feisal el Majali.
Owner: F. B. Klynstra

Documenta Hippologica

Darstellungen und Quellen zur Geschichte des Pferdes

Founded by
Col. H. Handler, Col. W. Seunig
Dr. W. Uppenborn, Dr. G. Wenzler

Edited by
Brigadier K. Albrecht, Spanische Reitschule, Vienna
General P. Durand, Cadre Noir, Saumur
H. J. Köhler, Prof. Dr. E.-H. Lochmann,
E. v. Neindorff, Dr. B. Schirg

1990
Olms Presse
Hildesheim · Zürich

Foppe Bonno Klynstra

Nobility
of the Desert
The Arab Horse of Bedouins

Translated from German
by Kathleen Schmitt
and Sigrid Eicher

1990
Olms Presse
Hildesheim · Zürich

ISBN 3-487-08318-3
ISSN 0175-9108

Contents

PREFACE

The noble Arabian breed by number comprises only a small part of the world's horse population. Its origins will probably always be a bit shadowy and might therefore be undervalued. Even horse breeders well-versed in general equine history are seldom up-to-date on the classic contributions over the last centuries of the Arabian's genetic strength and potency in founding and improving our developed breeds. So it is not surprising, in these fast-paced times, that this field has also suffered from a certain stagnation, and that breeding Arabians has been reduced in part to a sport, a hobby of the rich, an unproductive enthusiasm for the creatures' beauty and physical perfection.

Such opinions certainly invite dissension. Lightly said, they may possibly denigrate the breed in the public eye, or else distract and mislead some breeders. The author – a well-known biologist, expert on Arabians, and journalist – addresses these viewpoints in this comprehensive presentation offering a wealth of old and new documentation. Out of a deep conviction, he pits fact against prejudice, and focuses on the most important issues. His extensive knowledge and research are evident in his writings. By necessity they encompass all questions which concern the Arabian: from its first appearance in the desert, and the breeding practices so strongly bound to Islamic doctrine; to the influence of desert hardships on the health, the constitution, and the character of both the men and their deeply beloved horses; and, further, to the Arabian's own descendant – the English Thoroughbred. He traces the Bedouin's breeding methods, which are rooted in their religious doctrine of purity of blood among their own Bedouin clans, and then draws the parallel to an equally strong inner duty to produce asil, i.e., purebred, horses. It is clear that neither aesthetics nor a romantized love of beauty determined the Bedouins' breeding system. Rather, the demands of purity of blood and consistent performance in desert environs often decided on the Bedouin's life or death, wealth or poverty.

The author dedicates this book to his desert mare, NIJMEH, the ownership of which he attributes to a happy coincidence. Knowing NIJMEH, gathering impressions during his extensive travels, and being inspired by the asil horses' pride, nobility, and performance, his convictions were repeatedly confirmed by practical evidence. These experiences impressed him deeply and gave him the strength to fight, in word and picture, for the Arabian's often misunderstood nature. The Arabian has been known since ancient times as an elite, high-performance animal. Therein lies his true nobility! This must be maintained, and therefore we must also maintain the Bedouins' breeding methods, proven over thousands of years. He who believes these methods can be ignored, mixing precious pure blood with that of less well-bred stock, understands neither the spirit nor the purpose of these creatures. It is no wonder that the author judges breeding by the criteria of performance, hardiness, endurance, and prepotency, and teaches that our cliche's of beauty are not always appropriate. He argues passionately against self-destructive breeding of show and park horses and spoiled, barn-kept pets, which, having become soft, no longer deserve the name, "Arabian."

In all areas of the world, various tests and comparisons have demonstrated that asil, purebred Arabian performance horses measure up very well against the English Thoroughbred and other breeds in the toughest competition, track races, distance rides, and punishing tests of a horse's constitution. Selecting these horses, seeking out the very best strains, avoiding mixing them with mere show ring beauties, and increasing genetic uniformity and prepotency by occasional inbreeding – this is the way towards progress.

The urgent eleventh-hour task of far-sighted Arabian breeders is to collect and sustain the threatened but still available performance horse bloodlines, thereby renewing the breed's old brilliance.

The current critical situation forces the reader – whatever his individual viewpoint – to reflect, and to take a stand. It draws him into the exciting arena of the most important problems facing today's serious breeders and friends of these noble horses so indispensable for invigorating all horse breeds.

Dr. Georg Wenzler †
State Equerry, Ret.

CHAPTER I

THE FIRST HORSES IN THE NEAR EAST

The question is often raised whether our Arabian horses are directly descendend from wild horses that once inhabited the Arabian peninsula.

Archeologists' excavations indicate that horses, like elk and deer, were among the oldest of Man's companions. Food remnants from the early and late Paleolithic culture and Upper Paleolithic horse painting on cave walls in particular show that Ice Age Man knew of several equine types.

The strong, heavy Equus robustus lived in Holland, near the mouth of the Scheldt River, during the Pleistocene epoch (*Hooyer*, 1947), and Equus germanicus, among others, roamed Germany (*Lehman*, 1954), and so forth. They were not yet domesticated and were prey for the Upper Paleolithic hunters, at that time serving mankind as food. One could not really speak of horse husbandry or breeding in reference to this era.

The oldest finds indicating that man had domesticated the horse stem from the Tripolye culture on the upper Dnestr River, about 2500 BC. The wild Tarpan (Equus przewalski gmelini) lived there, in the forested Ukrainian steppes. The Tarpan lingered in the steppes between the Dnepr River and the Sea of Azov until 1880. He stood approximately 11 to 13.2 hands, was more slightly built than the Przewalski horse (Equus przewalskii polyakov), and was more refined from an equestrian viewpoint. However, his head was coarse, the skull being of medium breadth, but especially remarkable because of the concave rather than convex profile and the short muzzle (*Antonius*, 1918). Horses were supposedly first domesticated from these herds of Tarpans about 2500 BC. Horse breeding developed independently in the Altai mountain region of Siberia and in Iranian-Turkish areas as well.

What was it like in the Near East at that time? We know that there were no true horses south of the Caucasus Mountains then. Here, equine evolution ran a different course: instead of wild horses, Asian asses of the Equus hemionus group had evolved (*Antonius*, 1918, 1937; *Hancar*, 1955). Equus hemionus, the donkey, is not to be confused with the hybrid of horse and donkey – the mule.

Among the hemionus were the Kiang, the Chigtai in Manchuria and Siberia, the Kalan in Afghanistan and the western Ural mountains, the Onager in Anatolia, and the Hemippus

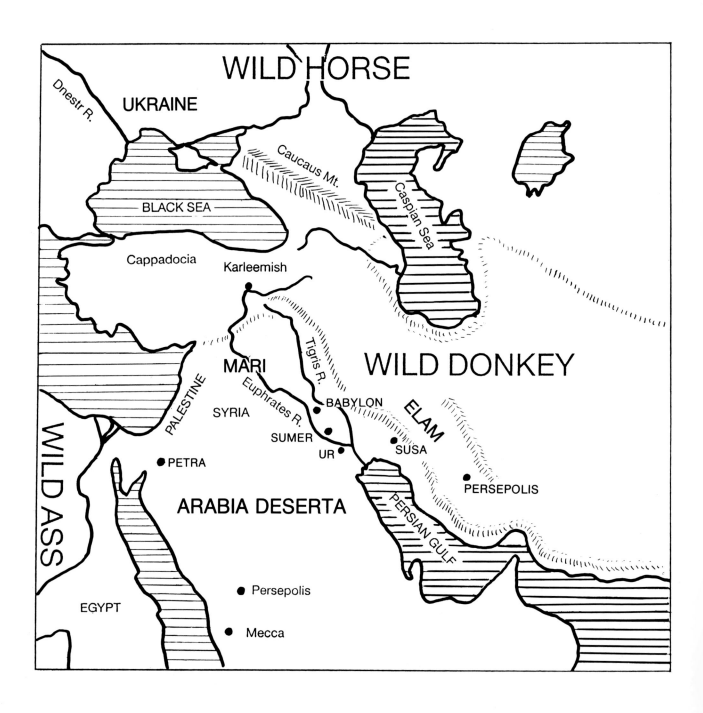

or half-horse (Equus hemionus hemippus Geoffr.) in Mesopotamia and Syria. Hemippus is especially important for us, since it was often confused with the true horse, despite the fact that it belonged to the hemionus group. Hemippus was domesticated by the Sumerians long before the true horse was imported into Mesopotamia. Xenophon knew of small "half-horses" running in huge herds, but we must consider them totally extinct today. Modern firearms in the hands of the Shammar and Anazah Bedouins were their demise.

Therefore, Hemippus, with its donkey tail and upright mane, was native to the Near East. Archeological discoveries will tell us when and how the first true horses arrived in this area. We shall see that the horse must still have been unknown as of 2000 BC in the area between the Tigris and the Euphrates.

The frequently cited bone tablet (*Zeal*, 507) from Susa in the eastern mountains of Iraq has caused much confusion. Dated from about 2800 BC, the engraved bone shows nineteen equine heads of assorted profiles and manes, and accompanying proto-Elamic writings. Initially, the heads depicted were taken for horse heads. Some authors even went so far as to say that these bone carvings represented the oldest pedigree of an Arabian horse (*Amschler*, 1933). True, some of the heads show a concave profile, but this is found in donkeys as well as Arabians. Antonius argued that they represented the Near Eastern donkey with its upright mane.

That interpretation is supported by a further archeological find, a stone tablet with cuneiform writing engraved on it – a page of book-keeping from King Bur-Sin of the Third Dynasty of Ur (2066–1955 BC). It accounts for 78 teams of four "Ansu" of all ages and types in the royal stables. "Ansu" was the Mesopotamian word for donkey. The horse, therefore, must still have been unknown in Mesopotamia around 2000 BC, or surely this king would have had some in his stables. The earliest proof of the true horse's arrival in the Tigris-Euphrates area dates from 1800-1700 BC. The first reports of horses here are found in old cuneiform texts engraved in stone tablets from this period. The animals were totally new to those people, as evidenced by the fact that they had not yet devised a word for these new "articles of import." "Horses" were referred to as "Ansu-Kura," meaning "Ass of the Mountains" (*Hancar*, 1955).

For a cultural/historical evaluation of this fact, recall that many west African jungle tribes called horses "Cows of the Whites" when they were first introduced by European colonists (Staffe in *Hancar*, 1955, p. 456).

Use of the term "Ansu-Kura" during this period points up the fact that horses were newly

Equine heads (Zeal 507),
engraved in bone, ca. 2800 B.C.
From the Suza finds

acquired, and brought in from the mountains. This is in complete agreement with archeological discoveries near the upper Euphrates, in the eastern mountains of Turkey. Three finds there indicate that as of 1950 BC, chariots drawn by true horses were already known in that area.

By 1700 BC, the city of Karkemish on the upper Euphrates was a lively center of horse-trading. This, too, is proven by stone tablets, one of which is in the form of a very primitive cuneiform letter from Aplachandas, King of Karkemish answering Zimri-Lin, King of Mari, a Mesopotamian city on the-mid-Euphrates as follows:

"White horses for the chariots are not available. I want to send out and, from there where they are available, have white horses herded up here. Until then, I will have blood bay horses brought in from Charsama."

King Aplachandas' stone tablet letter is of great interest to us, as it constitutes the oldest document in which white horses are specified. This indicates that, by 1700 BC, it was known how to breed for white or bay horses. The color grey is unknown among wild horses such as Tarpans or Przewalski horses. Therefore, horse breeding had reached a certain height by this time.

In Palestine, horse-drawn chariots were also known about the year 1700 BC, as shown by old fortress ruins of this period. These so-called "wagon castles" were especially built to accommodate chariots and their teams. In Egypt, on the other hand, the horse had not yet become a common item. It is generally assumed that the horse was brought to Egypt by the Hyksos. The Hyksos had once inhabited Syria and Palestine, but were driven out by chariot warriors, the Hurrains, whereupon the Hyksos banded together into a well-organized army, conquered the Nile delta, and stayed there for about a century (*Hancar*, 1855).

There are many archeological finds from this period, but none indicate that the Hyksos originally – i.e., about 1670 BC – used horses. They were probably forced to flee before the chariot warriors precisely because they still had no horses.

In Egyptian history the horse was first mentioned during the Wars of Liberation, 1580-1557 BC, when the Pharaoh Ah Mose engaged chariots to push back the Hyksos. It was then that Egyptians became truly familiar with horses – about 1000 years after horse husbandry had begun under the Tripolye culture in eastern Europe.

The oldest representations of horses in Egypt are found in XVIII Dynasty (1570 – 1314 BC) pharaohs' graves near Thebes. These horses had been gifts to the Egyptian pharaoh. According to paintings, they must have been quite small – perhaps 10.2 hands.

Horse remains from this period support this estimate. A mummified horse was unearthed forty years ago near Thebes from the grave of Queen Hat-Shepsut's protegé, Sen-Mut (1490–1468 BC). The horse, completely wrapped in linen, lay in a coffin just slightly under eight feet long. Under the linen wraps, the horse still carried a primitive saddle and girth. This had been a saddle horse, a young mare about 5–6 years old, about 12.2 hands, with a typical Arabian head. The vertebrae count went as follows: 18 thoracic, 5 lumbar, and 14 tail. Very probably we see here the remains of a horse that can be counted among the ancestors of the modern Arabian horse (*T. Chard*, 1937).

We still do not know how and when the horse came to the steppes and deserts of the Arabian peninsula. However, for zoö-geographical reasons, we cannot assume that the Arabian is traceable to any wild horse in Arabia. Perhaps some feral horses lived in Arabia, like the

American Mustang today, but these were surely not true wild horses. As far as known, no wild horses lived south of the Caucasus, that being the territory of the donkey.

No, the Arabian desert horse could only have been imported from the surrounding lands. As we have seen, horses were established animals in Mesopotamia, Syria, and Palestine as of 1700 BC, and also in Egypt as of about 1580 BC. These horses came from the north, having been imported over the Caucasus and other areas with several centuries of breeding history already behind them.

These were most probably traceable to Tarpans from west of the Volga.

The head of a Tarpan foal, as can be seen at the Duisburg Zoo, has a concave profile like that of the Arabian foal, and this may be an interesting point. It is unthinkable that the Ukrainians, living thousands of miles to the north, transported wild Tarpans over the mountains so that Arab nomads could breed Arabian horses. There is no basis for the hypothesis that the wild Tarpans could have been the direct ancestors of the Arabian horse. It seems much more logical that horses from the Mesopotamian, Syrian, Palestinian, and Egyptian breeds were the ancestors of our Arabian horses. The eastern Arabian Bedouins could have brought horses in from Mesopotamia, while the northern Bedouins got theirs from Syria and Palestine, and the westerners from nearby Egypt. Additionally, these countries were already in possession of highly-bred horses. Could this not be the basis for the existence of the three main types: Kuhaylan, Saqlawi and Mu'niqi?

It was not until many centuries later that Arabia could boast of much horse stock worth mentioning. In 450 BC, the Greek historian, Herodotus, relates that Bedouins under the Persian flag fought against the Greeks from camelback, and rode no horses. It is well known that horses have the advantage over camels in battle against infantrymen. One may conclude, therefore, that Arabic equitation had to make do without horses at that time. This assumption is supported in writings by the well-known Strabo, who lived during the time of Christ. Describing Arabia Felix, he wrote that there were no horses, mules or pigs there, and that Arabia Deserta had no horses – camels took their place.

The first sure report of Arabian horses comes from the 2nd century AD. Oppian, a Greek poet of that time, mentions them first as being rumored as good for hunting. Whether many or few horses lived in Arabia then is unknown, but it appears that the stock was not numerous. Arrian assures us that at this time horses were still being imported from Egypt into southern Arabia, brought there as gifts to the kings (*Ammon*, 1834, p. 89).

Not until the 4th century AD were horses available in Arabia in great enough numbers to partially substitute them for camels.

Ammian writes (*Marcellia*, XIV, 4, 8 and XII, 6; *Ammon*, 1834, p. 90): "The Saracens (a nomadic people of northern Arabia – Author) make all their raids on camelback, or on light, unpretty, but durable horses." In another place, he writes: "The Saracens are known everywhere for their fast, slim-bodied horses."

According to this account, then, northern Arabia during the time of Ammian did indeed have horses, but they were certainly no beauties. One must remember, though, that even Carl Raswan confesses in his book, *Drinkers of the Wind*, that he could not recognize the desert Arabians' beauty in their starved, coarse, ungroomed condition among the desert

Bedouins! "I was aghast! The truth slowly dawned upon me. The shock of the beauty of these creatures was followed by the realization that they had once been the same poor, shabby, disheveled horses which I, in my ignorance, had disdained at Nuri's camp and among the tribes of the inner desert." (*Raswan*, 1942, p. 278 – American edition).

If, in the 4th century, horses were rather scarce in northern Arabia, this was also the case in the south. In the year 344, the Roman Emperor Constantius presented the King of the Amorites, who ruled part of Yemen, with 200 Cappadocian horses, which were then as famed as the modern Arabian is today (*Ammon*, 1834, p. 91).

It is certain that during this time shortly before Mohammed, the breeding of Arabians developed rapidly; it is also quite possible that there were already blooded horses at that time. The Arabian poet Imru said: "We inherited this excellent race (the blooded horses – Author) from our forefathers, and our sons will own them after our death." (The Mu'Allagat, or the Golden Odes, the seven pre-Islamic poems displayed on the temple in Mecca.)

These old reports indicate that horse breeding in Arabia first reached its bloom between the 2nd and the 6th centuries – many centuries later than in the surrounding countries.

One wonders why horse breeding developed so late in Arabia. It would seem to me that the Bedouins' prior possession of such outstanding beasts of burden as their camels is responsible. The camel by its very nature would be better adapted to desert life than the horse. This would be especially true if the horses were not yet used to the hard desert life, as those of the surrounding highly-cultured lands certainly were not. For centuries, these horses had been kept in luxurious stables and fed generously. There had been no culling by the hardest of living conditions. And life in the desert is very hard indeed.

In the 20th century, the foal mortality rate stands at 50%, even for the Bedouins' fully acclimated desert horses. The mortality rate must have been tremendous for horses newly imported to the desert, breeding under equally hard conditions. Initially, hardly any breeding stock could have survived – only the strongest could have withstood the Bedouins' murderous demands. With these few strongest of the strong, the Bedouins would have been forced by circumstances to resort to inbreeding and even incest breeding.

So it is easy to understand why the old camel riders of the desert hesitated to raise horses. The risks were too great, and feed too scarce. Therefore, breeding stock was only rarely imported. Considering the high mortality rate, it is easy to estimate how long it must have taken to build from the few survivors a herd which was even to some extent genetically able to pass on the prerequisites indispensable for nomadic life in the desert.

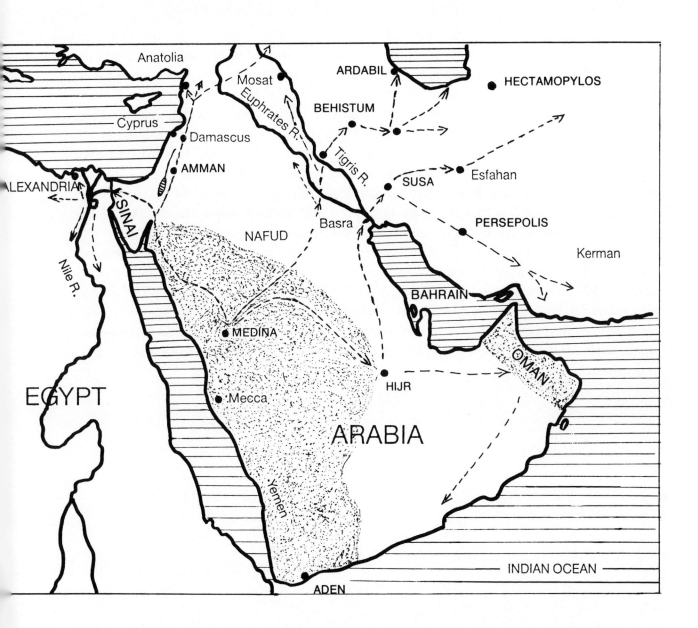

Anatolia

Cyprus

ALEXANDRIA

SINAI

Nile R.

EGYPT

Mosat

Euphrates R.

Damascus

AMMAN

ARDABIL

BEHISTUM

HECTAMOPYLOS

Tigris R.

SUSA

Esfahan

PERSEPOLIS

NAFUD

Basra

Kerman

MEDINA

BAHRAIN

OMAN

Mecca

HIJR

ARABIA

Yemen

INDIAN OCEAN

ADEN

Area occupied by Mohammeds
Troops in 632 A. D.

- - - - - -

Lines of attack of the Mohammeden
armies led by
Abu Bekr, Umar and Uthman

What was the condition of horse breeding in Arabia at the end of the 6th century? At the time, the Hejaz, the strip of land along the Red Sea where Mecca lies, was known for its horses. However, they must not have been numerous. In the northwest, in Arabia Petraea, there were many camels but also few horses. The interior, however, was rich in horses. The Bedouins of that time were the great breeders of the Arabian horse. The Banu Dhubyan, the Banu Taghlib, and the Banu Abbas tribes, among others, were famed for their superior horses. According to the early Arabian poet, Zuhayr, the Sheikh of the Banu Dhubyan owned a thousand lovely horses with magnificent fittings. Imru wrote that the Banu Taghlib's horses stood second to none in beauty and ancient origin. In the Hejaz, the Quraysh tribe had an excellent reputation for their horses (*Ammon*, 1834, p. 97).

Ammon sketched the following image of the Arabian horse, developed from several accounts by Arabian poets: *"They had a small head and a long neck; their back and croup were straight (the poet, Amralkais, said their backs were as smooth as the stone on which one rubs salves for brides); the body lean; the limbs lovely and strong; the feet fine but tightly built; the tail long and beautiful; and the coat short and fine. At the same time they were quick, swift, strong, durable, courageous, and undauntable, and as good for use in battle as in the hunt."*

CHAPTER II

BREEDING ASIL AS A RELIGIOUS OBLIGATION

Although the Arabian peninsula at the time of Mohammed's birth already claimed a blooming horse industry, we should begin the history of the modern Arabian horse breed with Mohammed's appearance as a prophet. In fact, it is difficult to view the Arabian horse apart from Islam. It was the prophet himself who made it almost a religious duty to breed asil desert horses. *"The Prophet Mohammed was foremost among the Arabs who cherished Arab horses. He was attentive upon them, seeing that they were well treated. Indeed it was his pleasure to listen to their neighing. He forbade crossbreeding, fearing purity's corruption, and knowing that once lost, it could never be regained."* (From the Arabic according to Omar Abdel Aziz in *Hamdan Stables Stud Book of Arabian Horses*, Cairo, 1969).

To further his plans among the sons of the desert, Mohammed attached great advantages to the ownership and care of asil horses. He promised that *"an evil spirit cannot enter a tent where a pure-bred horse is kept."*

"When someone cannot comply with all his religious duties, let him keep a pure-bred horse for God's sake, and all his sins will be absolved."

"He who makes sacrifices and prepares a horse for the Holy War will be treated, in the other world, as if he had been a martyr." (According to Emir Abd-el-Kadr in *Daumas, The Horse of the Sahara*, Eng. trans.).

These are stong arguments for the pious Moslem to guard the purebred horses' asil blood. To understand why Mohammed placed so much value on asil desert horses, we must look for a moment at the history of Islam. Mohammed was born in 570 AD, a member of the Quraysh tribe. He lost his parents and was raised by his uncle, Abu Talib. From his uncle he learned to lead camel caravans over dangerous, almost impassable paths. A caravan leader travelling through hostile territory must have had quite exceptional attributes. Mohammed had them in high measure, and became a respected, well-to-do caravan leader.

In his free time, he began meditating on the slopes of Mount Hira. Often, he would stay overnight in a grotto there. During one such night, the Angel Gabriel appeared to him, saying,

A sight to the eye, a joy under the saddle:
TUFAIL (Kaisoon-Faziza)
Bred and owned by Olms Arabians
Hamasa Stud, D-6301 Treis/Lda.:
W.-Germany

"Mohammed, you are God's chosen one, and I am Gabriel." When the angel again appeared to him a few days later, Mohammed was convinced. This night has since been known as "al Kadar," the Night of Destiny. The future of a great part of the world was in fact decided on this Night of Destiny, as was that of our Arabian horse, as we shall see.

For three years after "al Kadar", Mohammed taught only family members and his nearest friends the basic precepts of Islam (meaning "submission") – namely, that one should submit oneself to the will of the one and only God. As of 612 AD, he began to preach publicly, preferably not far from the holy Kaaba in Mecca. This soon caused difficulties. Mohammed was threatened, his sons persecuted and murdered. The situation became unbearable, and in 622 Mohammed fled to the city of Jatrib. The Islamic calendar is counted from this flight, "the Hegira," or "Hijra," on Friday, September 20, 622.

In Yathrib, later called Medina (Madinat an-Nawab, City of the Prophet), Mohammed found warlike Bedouins receptive to the new religion. During the time that followed, Mohammed doubtless came to appreciate the great advantages of tireless, fast horses. He and his fanatic disciples earned their livelihood by raiding rich, well-guarded caravans underway to and from Mecca. Having previously been a caravan leader, he understood the profession well. He won much acclaim when he, 300 infantry, and 70 riders, successfully raided Abu Sufyan's heavily armed caravan in the spring of 624 near Badr. Fourteen Moslems fell, while Abu Sufyan lost 70 riders, and 74 were taken prisoner. The spoils were tremendous:

It should be remembered here that the Bedouins considered the "ghazu" (raid) and plundering caravans as a chance to perform deeds of renown and to gain status, even into our century.

Following the above episode, Mohammed carried the war to the surrounding heathen Bedouin tribes. Due to his great successes, he gathered one tribe after another to his flag. The number of desert riders in his army grew daily. As long as the battles were confined to the coastal area, the Hejaz, he commanded no more than two- to five-hundred mounted soldiers, but once he conquered central Arabia, the Nejd, his troops grew to 10,000 (*Ammon*, p. 97).

After his death in 632, the succession went to the warlike Abu Bakr, who soon conquered the rest of Arabia. War was declared on the Sassanid's Byzantine Empire, (Persia). The Arabs' commanding general, Khalid Ibn al-Walid, was one of history's most skillful field commanders. He was victorious over large, well-armed forces, and overwhelmed fortresses that had been thought impenetrable. The Bedouins had become the most powerful army in the world.

The star of Gleannloch Farms Las Palmas Arabian Horse Stud Mr. and Mrs. Douglas B. Marshall Barksdale/Texas, USA: MORAFIC (Nazeer – Mabrouka), 1956– 1974. Another of the great Nazeer sons who distinctly influenced the Egyptian breed of asil Arabians

Following Abu Bakr, the second caliph (steward), Umar, reigned from 634 until 644. Under his reign, Khalid Ibn al-Walid defeated Heraklios' imperial army in 636 near the Yarmuk River in present-day Jordan. With that victory, all of Syria fell into Arabian hands. In June of 637, the Sassanid capital, Ctesiphon, was captured by the Arabs' general, Saad. Caliph Umar declared Holy War, "jihad", against all unbelievers.

In 642, the Egyptian capital city, Alexandria, was taken. The victorious Bedouins pushed ever westward. In 844, however, Umar was murdered, and was succeeded by Caliph Uthman. Under Uthman, the Koran reached its final form, derived from "… writings, forgotten tablets, and men's remembrances" (*Sugano*, Amsterdam 1970, p. 46).

In the meantime, the Arabian army pushed still further west. Still during Uthman's reign, Tripoli in Libya was conquered. Tunisia, Algeria, Morocco and Spain followed. The armies pushed on over the Pyrenees and finally into the heart of France. In the east, they reached the banks of the Indus and up to Kashmir. These overwhelming victories, which had so quickly transformed the formerly inconspicuous Bedouins into a world power, were attributed to Allah's help, of course. But the Arabian army officers were well aware of their swift, practically tireless desert horses' inestimable value for the Holy War. Victory or defeat at that time depended largely on the quality of one's cavalry. Its role on the battlefield was quite comparable to that of the Panzer divisions in World War II.

Fully convinced of the Arabian horses' superiority, Mohammed and the caliphs had feared that crossing them with the great number of captured horses could well lead to the downfall of the Arabian desert horse. So it was impressed as strongly as possible on the Bedouins to keep the breed pure. Again I quote: "*Should one not be able to comply with all his religious duties, let him keep an asil horse for God's honor, and all his sins will be absolved … An evil spirit will never enter a tent where an asil horse is kept … He who has bred an asil horse for the Holy War will save his mater from the fire on the Day of Resurrection.*"

These are religious duties for the pious Moslem, but Mohammed and his generals did still more to uphold the simple soldier's belief in the superiority of the Arabian horse. For example, a Bedouin who rode an Arabian horse received a higher wage than others. Ammon (1834) relates the following on page 100 of his book:

"*When the Arabs divided up the spoils after the victorious massacre at Yarmuk in 636, each rider with a horse of Arabian breeding received twice the portion of those who rode horses from other countries or of other parentage.*"

So it stood in the 7th century, and so it remained through the centuries. This fanaticism for purity of blood was anchored in the religion, and was also carried forward in poetry, becoming an indispensible part of the Arabian culture.

In the 10th century, the Arabian poet Mutanabbi wrote: "Noble steed, whose dam was covered by a noble stallion. (Translated from the Arabic, *Ammon*, 1834).

To keep the race pure, "noble" (purebred) mares were allowed to be bred only by "noble" purebred stallions. Consistently executed, one then is breeding purebred (asil) whether or not studbooks are kept. It suffices to know that the dam as well as the sire is of a recognized blooded strain, i.e., Kuhaylan, Saqlawi, etc. In this respect, the Danish Neiburh's report in his famous book, *Descriptions of Arabia from My Own Observations, and Reports Gathered in the Country*," (1772) is of interest. On pages 162–3, he describes how the Bedouins did this 200 years ago.

"... Although the Arabians have had no registry of their Kochlani carried over some hundreds of years, they can, nevertheless, be rather sure of their parentage, since the mares are always bred in the presence of witnesses – Arabian witnesses. While it hardly disturbs the conscience of many Arabs to bear false witness, there is no instance of an Arab ever having falsely testified about the birth of a horse, since they surely know that their entire family would be exterminated should they deny the truth in this case. So, if a Christian owns a Kochlani mare, or is keeping one for an Arab, and wants her bred by a Kochlani stallion, he must also call in an Arab witness. He stays with the mare for twenty days, to be sure no common stallion has dishonored her. She is not even allowed to see a stallion or donkey in the distance during this period. At foaling, the same witness must again be present, and the certificate of birth will be written up legally within seven days. The witness receives a 'Benish' – i.e., a garment, for his trouble. No mare of the Kochlani race is intentially allowed to be bred to a common stallion, and if this should happen through carelesness, the resulting foal is considered a 'Kadish.' The Arabs may well allow a highly bred stallion to be crossed with a mare of unknown background, but the foal from that mare is also considered Kadish (impure). So wrote Niebuhr, two hundred years ago.

In this century, too, the breeding of mares took place in the presence of witnesses. Spencer Borden presents such a report in his well-known book, *The Arab Horse*, (1906): ". . . and among the Anazah not one single purely bred mare (koheilet) may be bred excepting in the presence of witnesses, who later testify that her offspring is bred asil, a son or daughter of a purebred mare."

Facsimile of an "Huj-Ja"

(an Arabic certificate for an asil Arabian)

This is a certificate:
We, whose signatures and seals stand below, Sheikhs of the Suwailimats, branch of the Aeniza Bedouins, swear by Allah
and Mohammed, son of Abdullah, with truth, under no duress, in regard to the horse, Ma'-a-shi 'Hash-sha-i, from the
Suwailimats: he is a bay with a mark on his head like the new moon; by our stars and fortune, his dam belonged to the
Wad-da Khir-san strain; and his sire to the Kuhailan Abujunab – the well-known strain. He is a breeding stallion. It is
also known to us that Khidhr the Agel had to pay 550 gha-zis (ca. 88 L sterling) for him. We have written this testimony
to the best of our knowledge and understanding

We can look in vain for the names of grandparents, etc., in the pedigrees received when purchasing a purebred desert Arabian. It is required, however, that a purebred Arabian dam's strain be mentioned, and the sire's name is often entered, as well.

The following is a text from a typical Arabian pedigree dated 1951. The original is hardwritten in Arabic.

"In the Name of God, the Most Merciful and Compassionate:

By the blowing chargers,
By the strikers of fire,
By the dawn raiders Blazing a trail of dust,
Cleaving through the enemy host."

Koran, Sura 100

We, the undersigned, Sheikh Sharari-el-Bahit, and Sheikh Shaher-el-Diab, and Sheikh Taher-el-Diab, hereby certify as follows:
The horse bought by Ajub Kanuk, the Teherkess, from Sheikh Shaher-el-Diab and taken to Beirut, was sold to Mr. Henri Pharaon, who named him Shatt-el-Arab. This horse is of the breed Siglawi Jidran and was sired by Abu Urkub from the el-Diab family's stud farm."

Three seals and signatures follow. The pedigree, we see, begins with a quote from the Koran, and explains that the dam was a Saqlawi-Jidran and the sire an Abu Urqub, a strain related to the Mu'niqi. The term "purebred Arabian" is missing on all these documents. Only asil strains are recognized there, as we will explore in greater detail in the following chapter.

We could now ask if this blood fanaticism which became a religious obligation under Mohammed is still alive in the Bedouin in the 20th century. I would like to present some opinions given by experts in the field, who carefully investigated the matter in person, i.e., in the Arabian desert with the Bedouins themselves.

I would like to refer to Dr. H. Seydel as our first expert. Dr. Seydel was awarded his degree in Breslau for his thesis, *Das arabische Vollblut (The Arabian Purebred)* after a study trip through Arabia in 1932. He determined, among other things, that "(t)he fanaticism of the Arabian nomads with regard to the ancestry of their horses is as truthful and reliable as our most exact records of birth."

Also quite interesting is the official Turkish Commission's report, which begins as follows:
"By commission of the Turkish government, we, the department heads of the Animal Husbandry Section of the Ministry of Agriculture, Nurettin bey and myself, made a study trip to

Syria and Iraq from October 19, 1933 to February 20, 1934, to investigate the present state of horse breeding in these areas,. . ."

On page 30 of this extensive report, we read:

"From the above mentioned comments it can be concluded that a great confusion reigns in Arabia today as to type; nevertheless, the existence of a true Arabian horse cannot be denied. The reasons for this are as follows: although the Arab may completely disregard type in breeding, he does lay great value on a purebred broodmare being bred absolutely only to a stallion which also belongs to a recognized strain, i.e. a stallion that is Shabbuh. This blood fanaticism is the main reason that pure blood is bred only to pure blood, and thereby the most valuable characteristics are maintained, and less valuable blood is rejected. It is thanks to this blood fanaticism, or, biologically expressed, this pure breeding within the purebred strains, that representative examples of Arabian blood can still be found today despite the primitive stable management and breeding conditions. For this reason, it is essential to know the strains generally recognized as purebred."

As our third expert, I would like to cite the American veterinarian, Dr. Fred Pulling. In 1947, under commission by the American Arabian horse breeder, Mr. Hearst, he travelled to the Middle East with the director of the Hearst stud farm, Mr. Preston Dyer, and with Mr. John Williamson, to purchase some desert Arabians. After the expedition, Dr. Pulling wrote – among other comments that *"All importers of Arabian horses to England and the United States, including the members of the recent expedition, agree that these horses in their native lands (ie. Arabia) have not changed since the early nineteenth century."* The American expedition visited, among others, the Rualla Bedouins in the Syrian desert, which includes parts of northeastern Jordan, southern Syria, and eastern Iraq. This tribe still owned about 500 horses which had been born and raised in the desert. It turned out that many of these horses had been bred pure in strain, i.e. asil Kuhaylan, Saqlawi, etc.

Pulling also determined that, as of 1947, no written pedigrees were known to the Bedouins, so knowledge of each horse's parentage rested solely on passing on information orally. The post-World War II Bedouins themselves knew only of the so-called "memory pedigree." That such memory pedigrees are completely normal for purebred Arabians bred in the desert seems quite strange to Western breeders. They are accustomed to their stud book system with "complete," written pedigrees. A blank in the pedigree of an imported desert Arabian's name is something beyond their understanding. There presently is discussion among some "experts" to close our stud books to all Arabians bred in Arabia on the assumption

that no pure-blooded horses are bred in Arabia anymore. However, this myth was also being circulated a century and a half ago in England. The German hippologue, Dr. A. Jaeger, wrote in *The Eastern Horse and the Private Stud Farm of His Majesty the King of Wuerttemberg* (1846): *"In England, the Arabian horse had fallen into total disrepute: one could no longer purchase any highly bred and superior horses there, it was said, as they had been exterminated in wars or were thoroughly degenerated."* (*Jaeger*, p 9). But history caught up with this false conception. A half a century after the desert horse's supposed extinction, the Blunts bought first-class horses in Arabia which laid the cornerstone for the world-famous Crabbet Park breeding.

Today, in the second half of the 20th century, as before, there are breeders in Arabia who consider it a matter of honour to breed asil purebred Arabians. Alexis, Baron von Wrangel, who lived in Arabia for years, wrote in *The Arabian in Arabia* (1966): *"Outside of a few Bedouin families, there are however but few studs where the purest desert Arabian horses are still bred and where the blood lines of mares and stallions are diligently studied in order to keep the race pure. One of these is the famous Egyptian breeding farm founded by Sultan (sic) Muhammed Ali over 150 years ago; another is the stud belonging to Sharif Nasser, an uncle of King Houssein of Jordan; and lastly a private establishment owned by Dr. Iskander Kassis of Aleppo. This noted physician is a fanatical friend of the Arabian horse and devotes all his energy to preserving the remaining pure strains of the desert bred horse. In his efforts he is most ably assisted by an American citizen, Mr. Thomas Weaver, professor at Aleppo College."*

With 300 broodmares, however, H. R. H. Sharif Nasser's purebred Arabian stud farm was many times larger than El Zahraa. Some were kept in the desert, as this Bedouin prince explained to me, to stimulate the love and admiration for asil-bred desert horses. Breeding asil Arabians was much more than a mere hobby for Sharif Nasser ben Jamil. For his branch of the Hashemite royal house, it was a centuries-old family tradition. Eight hundred years ago, these direct descendants of the Prophet Mohammed were breeding asil Arabians, first in the Hejaz, where they were feudal lords of Mecca, and, after 1919, in present-day Jordan. The ancient bloodlines are sacred to them, and asil breeding is a religious duty. The "theft" of the mare, WAHIDA, in 1958, after the murder of Nasser's nephew, King Feisal of Iraq, points this up. To rescue the old bloodline, Nasser did not hesitate to resort to horse theft: typical for the true Bedouin.

Still larger than Sharif Nasser's breeding facilities are those of the King of Bahrain, H.R.H. Sheikh Isa bin Suliman Al Khalifa. When the royal family of Al Khalifa from the Arabian peninsula occupied the Bahrain Islands in the Persian Gulf about 200 years ago, they brought with them a selection of asil horses from the Arabian desert. Largely as a result of the Bahrain Islands' isolation (area: 186 sq. mi.), these Arabs could easily preserve their old methods of pure breeding. The royal stables presently hold about 500 Arabians (*Dannah al Khalifa*, 1971). Breeding there is done in the old, traditional, desert way. The older desert Arabians imported in 1782 are strictly separated from those given as gifts about 200 years later. Egyptian Arabians, for example, are accepted only for racing (*Schiele*, 1972). The families are still bred pure-in-strain. So one can see pure-in-strain Dahmans, Kuhaylans, Kursans, and others.

An example of such a pure-in-strain Kuhaylan Arabian is found on page 37, Vol. VI, of *The Arab Horse Stud Book* (England) – the bay Kuhaylan Al-Maisan stallion, BAHRAIN.

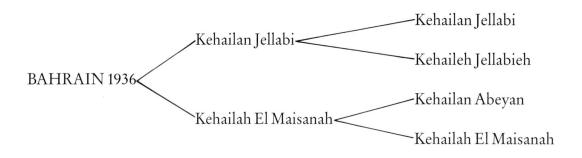

The oldest signs of Arabian horses in Egypt trace back to the 16th century B.C., as we saw in the previous chapter. However, the basis for the famous contemporary horse breeding there was not laid until the beginning of the past century. It was Mohammed Ali (Egyptian ruler from 1805 to 1848) who spent millions of pounds gold to build luxurious stables and to populate them with first-rate Arabian horses. Initially he bought them for top prices from tribal princes. Later, in the course of successful campaigns against the Wahhabi in central Arabia, he stole the best stock and sent them to his Egyptian stud farm.

Abbas Pasha inherited the precious horses in 1848 from his father, and expanded the collection with laudable expertise. After his death in 1854, the stud was disbanded. Many horses were sold, and some were sold abroad to France, Italy, and elsewhere. However, some of them did remain in Cairo. It was then that Ali Pasha Sherif took over the breeding program. His stud farm had about 400 horses, and he is generally recognized as the best breeder of classic Arabian horses in the second half of the 19th century. It was with this blood that the Blunts improved their own Arabian horses (*Raswan Index*, # 462, p. 29). Under Ali Pasha's son, however, the stud had to be publicly auctioned for debts.

In the West, now, it is all too often forgotten that the stock bred by Bedouins themselves has proven to be indispensible. In the first half of our century, too, knowledgeable Egyptian breeders fell back upon original desert blood. We can still see this in the Egyptian Arabians' pedigrees. One example of this is the pedigree of the stallion, SID ABOUHOM, foaled in 1936. Two of this stallion's four grandparents are "nameless" desert-bred (D.B.) Arabians. In the *Inshass Studbook of Arabian Horse Breeding*, we find numerous further such cases.

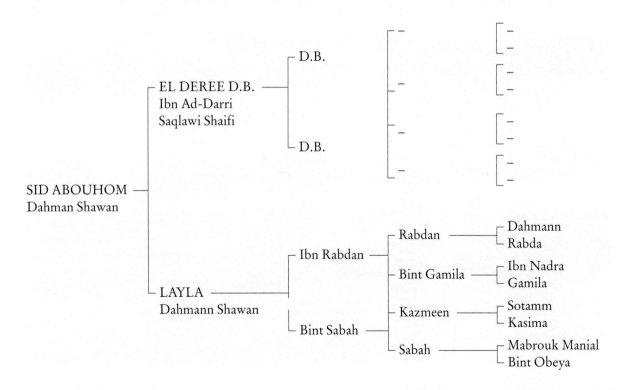

A wonderful chestnut mare with impressing gaits: BKA ALISABBAH (Ruminaja Ali-Glorietta Sabdanna)

Bred by Saluti-Birchknoll Arabians Owned by R. and C. Kristinus, Sundar Arabians, Villanova, PA, 19085–1101/USA Photograph: Sparagowski

These horses were often gifts from Bedouin princes, and were then used in the Egyptian stud. One example is the Kuhayalat mare, NAFA, foaled in 1941 in Saudi Arabia. Only her parents' strain names are entered, as is traditional (see Ch. III). Like many others, this desert-bred (D.B.) mare was used for breeding in Egypt where she produced 2 fillies and 3 colts. Her pedigree is blank behind her dam's name. We see another such blank in SID ABOUHOM's pedigree, and in that of many others. This is a riddle for Western breeders. Quite incorrectly, they assume in their ignorance that such a blank in a pedigree is an indication that the asil bloodline is unproven.

Although the English don't make it well known, they have often fallen back on original desert blood. Between World War II and now they have imported 28 desert Arabians, of which 9 were foaled after World War II, as a study of their *Arab Horse Stud Book*, Vol. VI (1944) and Vol. X (1970) will show.

They are:

Horse	Year Foaled	Breeder
Formidable	1945	Albu Asaaf Bedouins
Sabah	1946	Sheikh of Amara
Sabahia	1950	Sheikh Abdul Rezak, Iraq
Shammah	1950	Majali Bedouins, Jordan
Amal Al Sibaq	1954	Hadi al Hindi, Iraq
Comar	1954	Sheikh Habes el Majali, Jordan
Princes Mune	1958	Jordan
Shams	1955	Sheikh Habes el Majali, Jordan
Shamyl	1961	Habes el Majali, Jordan

Most of these come from Jordan. It cannot be coincidence that both desert Arabians entered in the Dutch Arabian studbook were also bred by the Jordanian Majali Bedouins.

| Misk A181 | f. 1958 | Majali Bedouins |
| Nijmeh A352 | f. 1954 | Majali Bedouins |

In the USA, on the other hand, most desert Arabians imported in the 1960's came from Saudi Arabia.

In the Arab countries there are few Bedouins who still breed asil horses. One of the few tribes with a significant herd is the Tahawi tribe in the Egyptian delta region.

Mrs. Erica Brunson, USA; the authoress, Erika Schiele; the Swiss journalist, Elsie Streiff; the breeder, Gustl Eutermoser; and, publisher and breeder Walter G. Olms are among those few who have interviewed the Tahawi Bedouins in person, and have seen their horses in the flesh. In day-long conversations with Sheikh Soliman el Tahawi and Mrs. Helga Tahawi, a German who has lived with the Tahawi for 20 years, as well as in my own lengthy discussions with Abdelati Abdalla Seoud, we were all convinced that the horses there are bred asil. The Tahawi uphold two aboulte principles:

1. Purity of Blood (el asil); and,

2. Performance

Type plays a subordinate role, so only about every tenth horse conforms to our idea of a typey Arabian. It is a difficult task for Egyptian and all other supporters of the asil horse to decide whether all asil horses should be internationally recognized, or should only the truly typey performance horses be accepted. El Zahraa could show us an example by using a few of the Tahawi's outstandingly classic performance horses, as the Hamdan Stables has done, supervised by the E.A.O.: FOLLA and her get, BINT FOLLA, FOL GAMIL, and MAR-SHALL; or as has done Mrs. Barbari, with a highly-bred Tahawi mare.

With the kind permission from the Swiss journalist, Mrs. Elsie Streiff, I quote the following, part of an article from her pen:

"The Tahawi Bedouins: Horse Breeders for Centuries

The nomadic life lies a good 200 years in their past, but for the sake of form and tradition, the Tahawi are still called Bedouins. Their ancient homeland lies in the present-day Saudi Arabian Hejaz. Three hundred years ago, they began the search for new pasture, moving through Libya and Tunisia and finally to Lower Egypt. There they served under Mohammed Ali, who as the sultan's governor in the early 19th century, held the country's fate in his hands. He rewarded them with generous sections of land. The later regent, Abbas Pasha, was so hostile to the foreign tribe that he threatened them with extinction. The Tahawi fled to Syria, and could return to their lands in the Sharkia province only after the regent's death in 1854.

Purity of blood.

Raising cotton, rice, and corn builds the solid basis for the Tahawi's established lifestyle. As Bedouins, they are unconcerned with propaganda and "recognized" papers for their horses;

as Bedouins, they have also maintained their conservative everyday lifestyle: houses are built only to receive guests. The wife furnishes the bedroom, dining room, and salon, but most of their life is not spent in these rooms. Traditionally, they sit separated according to gender on mats in the courtyard, and conduct their daily activities under the open skies. Their cuisine also has hardly changed since they abandoned the wandering life. Wage-earning black laborers perform the same duties that African slaves had done earlier. Week-long mounted field trips in the same natural elements encountered by their forefathers are among the most important events for these genuine sons of the desert. They are passionate desert falcon hunters.

The Tahawi sell their horses relatively cheaply, in comparison to the Egyptian Arabians, whose price has gone through the roof since they were discovered by American buyers. Much of their young stock returns to their parents' native Saudi Arabia or to Kuwait. The Tahawi Bedouins' horses are the offspring of those extremely durable mares and stallions whose ancestors accompanied them on their long wanderings out of the Nejd. This bloodline is adhered to fanatically. Not even breeding stock from kings and princes are recognized by the Tahawi. The Bedouins lay great value on a horse's ability to perform, a characteristic often known to have decided over the rider's life or death during their nomadic existence and on raids. They trade and buy horses only among themselves, since they trust only their own pedigrees. A mare's owner is always present when she is bred. He would entrust no one else with this duty. While Europeans, as a rule, take only beauty into consideration, no horse – however beautiful – would be used at stud if there is doubt about the most important criterion: "el asil" – purity of blood. Only the absolutely pure are recognized. In second place follow performance and beauty, although the Bedouins' "beautiful" horses don't necessarily appeal to European tastes. Written documents of parentage are not kept. It was emphasized that every Tahawi horse breeder can recite all of his breeding stock's maternal and paternal lineage with no gaps. The Tahawi do not spoil their purebred horses. All are hobbled, as is customary for other draft animals – donkeys and camels. Mares are bred at 4–5 years of age. Their foals are petted frequently from their first day of life, and cajoled with sugar lumps into accepting the presence of people – a psychological preparation for weaning at four or five months, if the dam is again in foal. The young horse is then tied to a four-to five-yard long rope by a neck collar. For the first few days he always has human company, which distracts and calms him in his new station in life. He is repeatedly touched and spoken to. A few weeks later, he, too, is hobbled. Before being led to water, the forehand and hindquarters are handled. In the seventeenth month of his young life, a saddle is laid on his back for the first time, and a little later one of the family's boys, about ten years old, will begin riding him. "I am always amazed how gently and trustingly the young horses behave for this," said Frau Helga el Tahawi, a native German and wife of 20 years of Sheikh Soleiman el Tahawi. Integrated into the traditional "resident Bedouin life" she officiated as translator of topical information. Since ages past, she explained, the tales of purebred, durable horses have been told among the menfolk as they gather in the "hair houses," as the Bedouins call their goat hair tents, and pass around a pot of their black, rather bitter coffee. Copper chestnut is the preferred color. Sheikh Soleiman had her translate an orally passed on theme: "All other horses are but servants to the chestnuts. They are like the princess, served by slaves, and it is they who can fly. Believe it, they are the daughters of the wind, and that is no exaggeration."

– Elsie Streiff

Unfortunately the efforts of the Tahawy were doomed to failure: Neither to EAO (Egyptian Agricultural Organization) nor the WAHO (World Arabian Horse Organisation) would register the Arabien horses bred by the Tahawy as pure-bred, with no exception of those few Tahawy descendants owned by the Hamdan Stables and by Mrs. Barbary (see above).

Odd and sad as it is: While the asil stock of Tahawy horses was not acknowledged, the probably non-asil Skowronek descendants in Egypt were acknowledged as pure-bred by the EAO and the WAHO.

Certainly there are skeptics here and there who, for whatever reason, question the oral tradition and therefore the asil horse, the desert-bred with strain names given for the sire and dam. "Who can say, given the completely different mentality of the East, that horses' pedigrees, above all, are supposed to be so correct, since it is surely possible to obtain many a lovely paper with seal and signature for the appropriate "baksheesh'?" it is said' and "we Europeans with our 'document delusion' are laughed at, and are given what we asked for with no great twinge of conscience. And the desert thieves, who have made their living from theft – why should precisely these same people be reliable in such an important matter? They are dreamers, those who would believe that!"

All skeptics and all interested parties are referred to the Asil Club's documents (see pp. 38-53) of which, for example, it is said in *South African Arabian:*

"No better collection of expert opinions of our horses will be found in the whole of literature dealing with Arabians."

An asil stallion from the Tahawy Bedouins.
The proud breeder and owner: Sheikh
Soliman el Tahawy from Sharkia, Egypt.

This collection of testimonies from literature regarding the Arabian horse convincingly presents the facts of the matter. If one cares to investigate further, references to the original works are given on page 301 of the above mentioned book.

To reaffirm this position, I would like to cite yet another author who, independent of any horsemanly prejudice, wrote the following in his excitingly-told book, *Verrat in schwarzen Zelten*, (Zürich, 1977), dealing with experiences of the Swiss gentleman, John Henry Mueller:

It was good to ride with these experienced men of the desert. To be sure – the inexperienced should not even attempt it. The Bedouin life is oriented toward survival, and for over a thousand years the leading families in Mecca, Medina, and Damascus have sent their sons to their desert tribes. There the youths become men: they learn about hunger, thirst, and survival; they are schooled with weapons and camels, instructed in the art of raiding and in desert diplomacy; and they are imbued with the desert's own code of honor. They are taught the traditions in such a manner that they will never be forgotten to the end of their days. Here in the desert, among the true Arabian aristocrats, they learn the meaning of keeping blood pure and the strict ban on marrying beneath their station. Their tribe's ancestory is learned as thoroughly as the Koran; these sons of the great families could unhesitatingly recite the names of forty generations. Here, they learn to abide by the Koran's requirements and to respect the thousand unwritten taboos of the desert.

For the great families' young men, this time with the desert tribe is a long and thorough purification process. By the end they will have become sinewy, strong men, cunning, hard as steel, and brutal, familiar with the ways of desert folk – the unconquerable well of strength for the family – with their power and strength as well as their own faults and weaknesses and those of their tribal comrades. They have been instructed in Arabic eloquence and verse, have built a tremendous vocabulary, and are well – versed in all forms of behaviour and etiquette. For over a thousand years, Arabia has isolated itself from the world, and during these thousand years, nothing in the central tribal lands' Bedouins' means or manner of living has changed; their dogged clinging to tradition and the Koran is a living anachronism in the 20th century. The Caliphates in Baghdad and Cordoba went to ruin because they grew soft, losing the conquered lands which once had comprised the greatest empire the world had yet known. But in inner Arabia, the desert's inhabitants' strength has remained intact, the people untouched by global developments, protected from all outside influence by the impassable isola-

tion. There is here still a kernel of that earlier tremendous power that conquered half the world and converted large sections of the Earth to Islam...

Now, not many exciting things happen in the Bedouin's everyday life, and a life among camels in the desert is not exactly strewn with sensation. So the Bedouin is wont to fall back on events of past years, engraving them on his memory as if on a copperplate. It is simply unbelievable how good a Bedouin's memory is and with what exactitude he can portray events of ten years ago. Not the smallest detail is left out, not one name missed, and he still remembers very exactly that he drank milk from a wooden cup decorated with brass nails in a star pattern. He may even know how many nails there were...
It is not unusual for Abu Chdeir to expound for four hours in the desert on the advantages of the Rualla camel saddle, but not yet cover half of the aspects important to a Bedouin."
(With the kind permission of the Schweizer Verlagshaus AG, Zurich).

The author of probably the most exhaustive and greatest work about Bedouins, the learned Max, Baron von Oppenheim, says in his three-volume tome, *The Bedouins*, (Leipzig, 1939-1952):
"The one truly binding thing, the one power before which the true Bedouin bows, is public opinion – fear of others' censure and mockery. Public opinion stands behind the unwritten desert code of honor that every Bedouin must respect."
Although Egypt is not of the Arabian peninsula. Its population is mostly Islamic. The famous state stud farm and breeding facility for asil Arabians is El Zahraa, in Cairo near Heliopolis, which is supervised by the E. A. O. (Egyptian Agricultural Organization, known as Royal Agricultural Society until 1949, founded in 1898). The exact translation of the stud's title is: Stud for the Breeding of Asil Arabian Horses: El Zahraa (Mahatet Tarbiat Al Konal Al Arabia Al Aseela 'El Zahraa').
Note: Arabians are bred there – asil Arabians – not Egyptians. One could say 'straight Arabians' per the English usage but it is perhaps better to use 'asil,' as every Arab would when he means 'pure.'
General Tibor von Pettko-Szandtner, previously commandant of the Babolna State Stud in Hungary, brought the stud (previously kown as Kafr Farouk) to a new brilliance in the 1950's. It was years, almost until 1970, before the world – especially the Commonwealth and the USA – recognized the value of these asil Arabians. These horses had been ignored for

decades, or even dismissed as degenerate, except among a few countries and private breeders who did successfully improve their breeding. Germany led the way, thanks expecially to State Equerry, Dr. G. Wenzler, who brought the stallions, GHAZAL and HADBAN EN-ZAHI to the state stud in Marbach, thereby leading the way for other great stallions such as KAISOON.

Here at El Zahraa was a sanctuary for maintaining Arabia Deserta Bedouins' valuable asil blood stock – especially that of the Nejd. They knew to add selectively the Bedouins' asil desert-bred performance horses to their stock, and did not hesitate to reimport asil stock or their get from England. So Egypt, too, lying in the same latitude as Arabia Deserta but with a completely different and milder climatic situation for breeding, clearly recognized the necessity of regularly introducing new blood from Bedouin stock.

One must differentiate between various Middle Easterners, especially urban dealers, and the Bedouins with their traditions, code of honor, and religious conviction. A Bedouin en-route to a 'ghazul' (raid) proceeds according to certain rules, is proud and hopeful of equestrian feats and adventures. He wants to prove his courage, and is characterized by his hospitality, conservatism in all matters of life, unconditional reliability, amazing memory, eloquence, and religious conviction. These qualities are absolute necessities in communal desert life. He who sins against them, and therefore against the requirement to breed with asil blood, is expelled from the community. He also lives in constant fear of punishment after death.

The great interest in asil Arabians now alive throughout the Western world must not lead to importing blindly everything merely because it is asil. Such a run on asil Arabians has contributed to importing horses from countries unrecognized by WAHO, or to buying stock from Egypt that was meant to be sold domestically at auction by El Zahraa, for example, and not to be exported. Caution is advised in acquiring such horses being detoured through dealers. Every stud farm, small or large, has culls which must be sold. Such culls, meant to be sold as saddle horses, must not reappear as breeding stock.

CHAPTER III

STRAINS AND TYPES

Everyone who has studied Arabian horses' pedigrees knows them. Strange-sounding Arabic names such as are found under the names of stallions and mares in the old *Studbook of the Netherlands Arabian Horse Club*, 1952: Hamdanieh under A35; Managhueh Ibn Sbeyal (A65); Koheilet Ajuz of Ibn Rodan (A28), Kohaileh Foershal (A137), etc.

Like many registries the Dutch studbook commission decided that strain names would not be included in the new Register A, of *Het Arabische Paardestamboek Nederland*. Yet I believe they are of interest, and I will devote a few pages to them, especially since they still do appear in pedigrees.

In the original lineage documents for purebred Arabians imported from Arabia, there is no explicit designation of the horses being purebred Arabian. As a rule, the pedigrees are translated into English. The sire's and dam's strain names are given, as explained in the previous chapter.

In the 8th century, one spoke of ARABI when referring to purebred desert horses, but the term KUHAYLAN was later substituted. 'Kuhaylan' is the diminutive form of 'kuhl,' the black coloring used by Arabic women to make up their eyes. It refers to the black color of the very thinly-haired skin around a highly-bred Arabian horse's eyes. It is especially noticeable in greys. It looks as if the eyes had indeed been made up.

The written rendition of Arabic words is by no means uniform. Whereas the Dutch may render a certain sound with 'oe,' the Germans use 'u,' and the English 'oo.' The Arabs pronounce 'h' much like a soft 'ch,' but this may be rendered in Western languages as 'h,' 'ch,' or 'g.' The Arabic also has masculine and feminine forms for words, so it is understandable that the written forms of the same word could vary sharply. One may therefore see the forms Koheilan, Kohaylan, Kuhailan, Kochlan, Koheilah, Koheilet, etc.

Although 'Kuhaylan' has been used to denote all pure-blooded Arabian horses, it is more truly the name of one of the five most famous strains or families among Arabians, which are collectively known as AL KHAMSA or 'the five:' Kuhaylan, Saqlawi, Abayyan, Hamdani, and Hadban.

*CL PRINCESS AMURATH
TURFA (Mascha Farag –
Hamasa Serra) is regarded as
the first asil filly combining
the famous bloodlines of
Amurath 1881/Weil, Turfa,
Fadl, Moniet el Nefous and
Nazeer. Amurath 1881/Weil
(35 x Bairactar-Murana I),
Turfa (the coronation gift of
King Abdul Aziz Al-Saud to
King George VI of Great
Britain)
Bred and owned by Corinn
Arabians Leuthäuser, D-8603
Ebern/W-Germany
Photograph: Escher*

Aside from these five famous families, the Bedouins recognize about a dozen others, though these are less valued. In the literature we often find that some other strains are counted among AL KHAMSA, and Mu'niqi often replaces the Hamdani or the Hadban. The other strains are (according to *Raswan*): Dahman, fem. Dahmah

Mu'niqi, fem. Muniqivah

Shuwayman, fem. Shuwaynah

Milwah, fem. Miluwiyah

Mu'wajj, fem. Mu'wajjiyah

Rishan, fem. Rishah

Tuwaysan, fem. Tuwaysihah

Abu 'Urkub, fem. Umm Urkub

Jilfan, fem. Jilfah

Kubayshan, fem. Kubayshah

Rabdan, fem. Rabdah

Sa'dan, fem. Sa'dah

Samhan, fem. Samhah

These strains are to a great extent related to each other however.

One could ask why the Bedouins separated their purebred horses into strains or families. Many a romantic explanation can be found.

The best-known myth is probably that of the Prophet and his thirsty mares. According to this legend, the Prophet corralled a hundred mares for a few days. A fresh mountain stream splashed quietly nearby, but the horses were not given a single drop of water. Finally, Mohammed opened the gates, and the thirsty horses galloped towards the stream, greedy for water. But before they could reach it Mohammed had his trumpeter sound the call to gather. Five mares left the herd without having drunk a sip, and galloped to the gathering place whinnying gladly. Despite their burning thirst they had obeyed their master's call immediately. With a blessing he laid a hand on their manes one after the other and named them ABAYAH, KUHAYLAH, SAQLAWIYAH, HAMDANIYAH, and HADBAH. These five mares, AL KHAMSA, are supposed to be the foundation mares of all genuinely purebred Arabians.

Less well-known is the legend reported by the Emir Abd el Kader el Gazairi in his book, *Al Safinat El Guiad* (Beirut, 1948): Long ago, when Yemen was afflicted with a drought, the horses fled with the wild animals to safer places. Their descendants appeared many years later in the Nedj, and were discovered by five Bedouins. The Bedouins could hardly believe their eyes. Overjoyed, they decided to capture some of these splendid horses. Day and night they watched them, to discover the well at which they slaked their thirst. Then, cautiously, they began to build a fence. At first, it was very wide in front, to allow the horses free access. When the horses first saw the fence, they were frightened, turned, and fled back to the desert. But that did not last very long. Driven by thirst, they returned, slipped through the wide opening, and drank their fill at the familiar well. In the course of the next few days, the men gradually narrowed the opening. The horses returned every day. After many days, the entrance was finally narrow enough for the men to close it quickly behind the horses. The trap was shut. There was no escape. With some difficulty, each Bedouin managed to catch a horse from the herd. Bareback, they started on their way back to camp. They had a long ride in front of them, and trapping the horses had taken so many days that their provisions were giving out. Starving, they rode on for a few days. They had just decided that they had no choice but to slaughter a mare, if they were to survive the adventure. Just then, a herd of gazelles came into view. In a flash they were after them. After a long chase, they hunted down one gazelle. As is customary at Arabian races, each mare now received a name. First in line was the lucky hunter's mare. This horse had exceptionally deep flanks, so she was named SAQLAWI, which means "the one with the well-formed flanks." The second, the one that had happened upon the prey, was named UMM URQUB, because of her deformed hock (Urqub = hock). The third one had a noticeable birthmark, and known thenceforth as EL-SHOUIMA or SHUWAYMAH. The fourth was named KOHEILAN. The last rider had lost his cloak (aba or abayyah) during the wild ride. But it hung from the mare's high-carried tail, so his mare received the name ABAYYAH.

So, Saqlawi, Umm Urqub, Shuwaymah, and Obeyah (Abayyah) were the five founding dams of the five families known as Al Khamsa according to this legend.

Of course, these are just legends, but they do show that horses' family names mean a lot to Bedouins. How old are these names? According to Schiele they must have arisen after the 14th century. They have certainly been in existence for over 200 years. Niebuhr, 1772, names Saqlawi, Hamdani, and Mu'niqi, among others. However, Dr. Abdel Alim Ashoub (1948) reports that these strains were mentioned in books by Al Asmai Abdel Malek ibn Koreib and by Abu Abeida Moammar el Mothny, born in 732 AD in Ragab.

Aside from these romantic legends about the origins of the various strains within the Arabian breed, there is little we know for sure. We know now that there originally were fewer

A mare of the Koheilan type, HAMASA (Hadban Enzahi – Shar Zarqa), winner of many a competition, twice best pure-bred Arabian bred in Hessia. Her offspring is successful in Germany as well as in Sweden

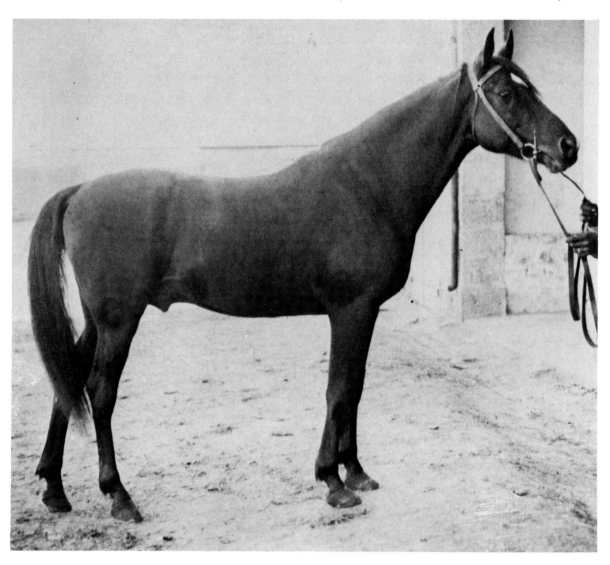

strains. We know, too, that horses in Arabia were originally imported from the surrounding countries: Mesopotamia in the east, Syria and Palestine in the north, and Egypt in the west. Horses were also imported from Cappadocia, as mentioned in Chapter I. These horses were probably of assorted breeds themselves. This may explain why there are assorted main types within the Arabian breed.

Now, Arabia has a huge area of perhaps two million square kilometers, mostly desert, barren mountains, and sparsely vegetated steppes. Only a few strips along the coast have ever supported any lush growth. The few wells in the interior are widely separated from each other. The extraordinarily sparse plant growth forced horse-, camel-, and sheep-breeding Bedouins to move around from one pasture to another. Each tribe therefore needed a lot of space – no other tribe was tolerated nearby. They could not be, if one didn't want to starve oneself. So Bedouins were forced to lead a very isolated life. Their horse breeding was also more or less isolated, although there was an exchange of breeding stock through trading and raiding.

Many Bedouin tribes were outstanding horse breeders, while some were less successful. Certain areas were more suitable for horse breeding. Climatic variations had an effect as well. Many an expert sheikh made his mark on the breed, as did the famous Sheikh Jidran ibn ed-Darri of the Qumusa-Saba Bedouins. He inherited Saqlawi mares from his father, Sheikh Darri. From these he bred an exceptionally good strain which he called the Saqlawi Jidran. In the course of time, from presents, theft, or trade, some Saqlawi-Jidran mares fell into the hands of Sheikh Sudan, Sheikh Subayni, and Sheikh Merghi. These carried the breeding forward more or less successfully. The Saqlawi-Jidrans they then bred are called:

    Saqlawi-Jidran of Ibn Sudan
    Saqlawi-Jidran of Ibn Subayni
    Saqlawi-Jidran Summi
    Saqlawi-Jidran Marighi

These names gradually shortened to Saqlawi Ibn Sudan, Saqlawi Marighi, etc.

This name is passed on from mother to daughter, regardless of whether a Saqlawi or Kuhaylan stallion was the sire.

The Kuhaylan strain is by far the most numerous, with about 100 sub-strains. Next come the Abayyan and Saqlawi, with about 24 sub-strains each. On the other hand, the Kubayshan has but one sub-strain. It would be too lengthy to list all the 200 or so known sub-strains here. If you are interested, refer to *Arabian Horses* by Raswan and Guttmann, or *The Horse of the Desert* by W. P. Brown.

Carl. R. Ras⋯
This n⋯
German n⋯
himself of ser⋯
to the Ara⋯
horse few c⋯
in the 20th cen⋯
have done⋯
lived for n⋯
years as a Bed⋯
amon⋯
Bedo⋯
Photogr⋯
Esper⋯
Raswan Arc⋯

After the hunt. Carl Raswan (middle) with his blood brother Emir Fawaz (second from left). To the right foreground, the prey: a gazelle. Photograph: Esperanza Raswan Archives

Carl Raswan (middle) with Emir Fawaz and Prince Aurans (Named by his father, Prince Sattam, after Lawrence of Arabia), who has here just been taken into the group of "Heroes and Horse Theives" in the Ruala tribe

41

Are there still differences between all these strains and sub-strains? Opinions on this vary widely. According to Dr. Abdel Alim Ashoub, Director of Cattle Breeding for the Royal Agricultural Society of Egypt in 1948, there should be absolutely no difference. H. R. H. Sharif Nasser ben Jamil is of the same opinion. During a conversation about this at his huge stud, Ruseifa, in Jordan, this excellent breeder demonstrated with his own breeding stock that it is in fact impossible to differentiate between a Saqlawi, Abayyan, or Kuhaylan on the basis of appearance. True, two definite types could be seen, but that was unrelated to strain name. Sharif Nasser called them the 'mountain type' and the 'sand-desert type.' The mountain type was smaller, their nostrils were much larger, and their coat coarser. The sand-desert type had longer legs and much larger, wider hooves, and a much finer, shorter, and shinier coat, and nostrils resembling those of camels. Apparently they were better adapted to desert dust and sandstorms. Of course, many horses showing traits of both types were to be seen, but that again had nothing to do with their strain. Quite in opposition to these explanations is the opinion of our famous expert, Carl Raswan, a German who went to the Middle East before World War I. He lived for many years as a Bedouin among the Bedouins, and indeed was blood brother to the prince of the powerful Rualla Bedouins. The purpose of his travels was to thoroughly study the Arabian horse. He left to us the whole of his knowledge in his 7-volume standard work, *The Raswan Index*. The seventh volume was published posthumously. He finished the book on September 24, 1966, exactly three weeks before his death. On p. IV of Vol. 7, he writes that "*...each strain name was chosen to express a distinguished type.*" What were the relevant characteristics?

1. *Differences in conformation (of the body) as width, narrowness, length, shortness, shape of barrel, croup. Differences in length or shortness of legs, width size, circumference of cannon bones.*
2. *Differences in shape of heads and certain characteristics (or lack of them).*
3. *Colour of hair (coat).*

According to Raswan:
KUHAYLAN – Strength. Deep and wide chest and hindquarters (as opposed to the feminine beauty of the Saqlawi). Rounded lines (as opposed to the angular Mu'niqi). Ideal saddle horse with tremendous endurance. Height – 14 to 15 hh.
SAQLAWI – Beauty. Femine elegance. Ideal show horse. The most beautiful of Arabians, yet very wiry. Head and tail carried very high. Head a bit longer than the Kuhaylan, and a

bit less broad between the eyes. Ears somewhat longer. Neck and back a bit longer than the Kuhaylan, too.

ABAYYAN – Similar to Saqlawi but carries the tail still higher and the back is a little longer. The legs recall those of a racehorse. Splendid shoulder and enormous ribcage (barrel chested). Often swaybacked. Very fast and exceptionally agile. Sufficient endurance. Ideal polo pony.

HAMDANI – Hunter-type. Large head with straight profile, broad between the eyes and less dry. Croup not straight. Height 14.2 to 15.2 hh.

DAHMAN – Very classic type, strongly resembles the Saqlawi. Head very wedge-shaped, short and broad, with a strongly concave profile. Eye exceptionally large. Color grey or chestnut, height 14.2 to 15 hh.

MU'NIQI – Speed. Long, narrow racehorse, strongly resembles the English Thoroughbred. Often coarse and common. Not at all classic type. Sloping croup, tail low set. Splendid legs.

So, in response to the question, whether or not the strain is indicated by external traits, opinions do vary widely. Did Raswan pull the descriptions of the various strains from thin air? To judge on the basis of the horses themselves, as I personally have seen in Egypt, Jordan, and Lebanon, it must be out of the question to tell a Kuhaylan from a Saqlawi by their appearance. But that was in 1972 – 1973. We must remember that Raswan was writing mostly during the pre- and post-World War I period, that is, about half a century ago. Raswan during these years saw the Arabian peninsula as practically no other European had seen it, saw and heard more than any tourist, because he lived as a Bedouin. They trusted him; he spoke their language, which was decisive. He sought out the old, orthodox breeders in the farthest reaches of the desert. He sat at the campfire with them, drank coffee in their black tents, conversed with his hosts about horses for hours. At least in part, his descriptions are of the old traditions and the experiences of the past century. But he also saw many a pure-in-strain horse, including the Rualla Bedouin Amir Sha'lan's Kuhaylan-Ajuz.

Judith Forbis, too, saw pure-in-strain Mu'niqis with the Bedouins on the Turkish – Syrian border in 1959. But these are exceptions. Today there are hardly any breeding programs which breed pure-in-strain. What we see today is not a measure of that which originally was. Raswan knew this in the bottom of his heart, and wrote on p. III of Vol. 7 of the Raswan Index: *It is of no use to go to the 'Wailing wall' in Jerusalem and cry with Israel about the lost glory of something that we cannot recover today anymore, because only some*

43

Siklawi type.
One of the great Nazeer sons in Europe,
of great merit on behalf of the breed
of pure-bred Arabians.
KAISOON OA (Nazeer – Bint Kateefa)

Champion Stallion of the Arabian Horse Show
at Celle, FRG in 1971. Born at El Zahraa,
owned by the Duisburg Zoo
Photograph: W. G. Olms.

old paintings and other objects of art are left to us which testify that there was once a special breed of horses, created in the inner desert of the Arabian Peninsula – a supreme type animated with the breath-of-Allah in every fibre of their glorious bodies and 'divine' heads."

Yet, today we still see here and there pure Kuhaylan, Saqlawi, and Mu'niqi types as described by Raswan, apart from mixed types or even very untypical Arabians. I am thinking of the Egyptian stallion, KAISOON, for example, who is presently at the Duisburg Zoological Gardens. This stallion embodies the pure Saqlawi type, but is a Kuhaylan. Another NAZEER son, HADBAN ENZAHI in Marbach, is a Kuhaylan type. The stallion's name is actually KAMEL, and he is a Hadban-Inzahi, Kuhaylan though he may look. The Egyptian mare, FOZE (NAZEER x FATHIA) is also a Hadban-Inzahi, but by appearance would be taken for pure Saqlawi. So, the strain types still exist today, but they are no longer bound to the strain name. The explanation for this is quite simple: we no longer breed with consideration for strain. Take, for example, the stallion SAWLAGAN, foaled 1968 at the Egyptian stud, El Zahraa. Sire: ALAA EL DIN; dam: MAHBOUBA. By tradition he is a Hadban. But a study of his pedigree shows that of his thirty-two 5th generation ancestors:

13 were Kuhaylan
 7 were Saqlawi
 5 were Hadban
 4 were Dahman
 1 was Mu'niqi
 1 was Hamdani

Another example is the stallion, MADAH.

MADAH was foaled in 1966 at El Zahraa in Egypt, by MORAFIC out of MAYSA, and was considered an Abayyan. Of his 32 ancestors:

11 were Saqlawi
 7 were Kuhaylan
 6 were Dahman
 5 were Hadban
 1 was Mu'niqi
 1 was Abayyah

With such a background, can it be expected that the Abayyan stallion would exhibit Abayyan characteristics as described by Raswan?

So we see that today no conclusion can be drawn regarding an Arabian's type on the basis of its strain name. But the strain name on a desert Arabian's pedigree and document is of great importance to breeders, since it is a guarantee that the horse is out of a "thoroughbred" desert mare, i.e., an asil Arabian. The greatest value of the strain names in analyzing pedigrees lies only in a negative sense: there is no guarantee of a desert-bred horse's purity of blood if its strain is unknown. Such a horse could be asil, but Bedouins would consider it to be "Kadish" if there were any doubt at all.

Examples of horses considered "Kadish" by the Bedouins are even found in *The Arab Horse Stud Book*. We see in Vol. 7 (1957) on p. 39: SAHIL, chestnut stallion, foaled 1942, desert bred, of unknown strain and unknown pedigree, breeder unknown. SABAH on p. 87; desert bred, of unknown strain and unknown pedigree, from Baghdad; KHIZIL, on p. 88, of unknown strain from Pakistan.

In older sections of the studbook we find many more examples. The stallion, ZOOWAR, in Vol. I, p. 79, probably carries the crown in this respect. The only thing we know about this horse is that he was a successful racehorse in India; strain unknown, pedigree unknown, age unknown, breeder unknown. No expert could consider such a horse a purebred. Dr. Houtappel also wrote: "The data for some "purebred" Arabians was largely unknown to me. This was why I cleared them out rather radically a few years ago, since ZOOWAR and CROSBIE were recorded in their pedigrees."

Not recording the known strains in the new edition of *Het Arabische Paardenstamboek Nederland*, Register A does not simplify analysis of Dutch purebred Arabians. It also breaks an old tradition, which is very much to be regretted.

Kuhaylan type.
FAZIZA (Fa-Turf – Azyya), a Koheilah
Jellabiah, whose maternal line traces back
to the legendary mare WAZIRA, the Feysul
Jellabiet.

CHAPTER IV

CONFORMATION

When we consider the breeding programs for particular breeds of dogs, we can assume that all breed characteristics which the dogs must show are clearly stated. At shows, the animals exhibited resemble each other down to the smallest detail. This is so for most show animals. All breed characteristics are strictly regulated. It would seem that this would be the case for the Arabian breed, also. This however is not the case. There are a number of types within the Arabian breed, as seen in the previous chapter. Judging by appearance, in fact, we see a number of "sub-breeds." Perhaps it would be more correct to speak of a very intermixed group of "sub-breeds." They are so intermixed because they have all been bred with the same goal in mind. The horse was to be capable of carrying a heavy burden – the rider – over difficult terrain under extreme climatic conditions as quickly as possible. Everyone had a desert war horse in mind, and the origins of the various types were largely the same.

While visiting the stables of the Marquis Mousse de Freige in Lebanon, this connoisseur of the Arabian related the following for our consideration: *"You Europeans make the great mistake of having the idea of but one type of purebred Arabian. Actually, there are almost two hundred different types."*

The estimate of "two hundred" types may be a bit exaggerated, but it clearly emphasizes that it is impossible to speak of a standard Arabian type. The Arabian purebred could be compared to the greyhound, in that both are bred for the same goal – performance – and both are specialized breeds, similarly built in some respects.

To complicate the matter further, some European countries have tried to develop their own types. Intermixture of bloodlines, climatic influences, and varying selection of breeding stock are most important bases for this process.

In the following descriptions of conformation, we must take these circumstances into account.

Arabian horses do not excel by their refinement only: Among other factors they possess fertility and longevity.
The picture shows 28 year-old FARAG (Morafic – Bint Kateefa) who is as healthy and vigorous as ever.
Bred by El Zahraa, Cairo
Owned by Olms Arabians Hamasa Stud, D-6301 Treis/Lda./W-Germany
Photograph: H. Reinhard

The Head

As a rule, the head is the highly characteristic feature of this breed. The Bedouins laid special value on three aspects: the forehead, the ears, and the juncture of head and neck.

The forehead, or jibbah, must be somewhat rounded between the eyes. Seen in profile, the forehead curves to about a third of the way down the face. Then there is a slight dip, giving the Arabians head its concave shape. The lower part of the nose curves up again slightly. The nasal bone is concave above, and convex below.

The convexly curved forehead is quite noticable in foals (see photo). This feature is less pronounced in mature horses. Only pure-in-stain Abayyans retrain the curved forehead into their old age, and it is more strongly curved in mares than in stallions. This type of forehead, so characteristic of Arabians, is lacking among Hamdanis and Mu'niqis, and their related strains. Their profile is straight.

Thanks to the forehead's curve and breadth between the eyes, the Arabian – especially Kuhaylans, Saqlawis, and Abayyans – has a larger cranial capacity than do other breeds. The brain is also relatively larger than that of warm- and cold-blooded horses. Reduced to a base common weight of 425 kg, we find the following brain volumes (according to Barahmi):

Belgian Coldblood	480 ml.
Trakhener	531 ml.
Purebred Arabian	655 ml.
Przwalski Horse	850 ml.

Arabians, we see, have a larger brain relative to their size than do other breeds developed by man, and is closer in this respect to the wild horse. The Arabian's forehead is broader than in other breeds, as was known by experts on the original desert-bred. According to measurements of European Arabians, the ratio between the length of head and width of forehead is as follows:

German Arabian	100:37.6
Polish Arabian	100:38.7
American Arabian	100:39.0 to 40.0
Spanish Arabian	100:40.0
Trakhener	100:38
Mecklenburger	100:37

So, German and Polish Arabians are narrower in the forehead than would be expected; also, the Polish Arabian's head is too long. The Spanish Arabian has better retained the short, broad head, and so appears more classic. The total length of the head reduced to a common base body size according to Flade (1966) and Pozo Lora (1958), is as follows:

Spanish Arabian	53.1 cm
German Arabian	54.8 cm
Polish Arabian	55.9 cm
Trakhener	57.0 cm
Mecklenburger	64.5 cm

The German Arabian's position just between the Polish and the Spanish Arabians is explained by the high percentage of Polish blood in German Arabian breeding.

The Ears

The second point by which a Bedouin judges a horse is the shape and carriage of the ears. The best examples of the breed have very elegantly formed ears which curve to a point so that the tips almost touch. The inner edge is sharply curved, and kinks to the inside near the tip. The ears should be lively and flexible, thickly furred on the inside to protect against desert sand. Mares' ears are longer and less sharply pointed than stallions. There are differences in the ears of various strains. The Saqlawi have longer ears than the Kuhaylan, just as those of the Hadban are longer than those of the Abayyan. The Hamdani on the other hand have very small ears.

The Eyes

The eyes must be large and expressive. They sit on the side of the head and stand out from the head a bit. This location ensures a good field of vision to the rear, which is of great importance for a preyed-upon animal such as the horse for quickly recognizing danger approaching from behind. The eyelashes are long and fine and slanted, unlike other breeds, whose eyelashes are short and straight.

The eye lies rather low in the skull. The distance from the upper edge of the nostril to the eye is only 3 cm longer than from the eye to the top of the head. In other breeds the eye lies 7-8 cm higher. This is typical of the breed, but is lacking among Mu'niqis, whose eyes are smaller and laid higher in the head.

*"The head almost gives the impression of
being made up only of eyes and nostrils."
Arabian mare FATIMAH (Fol Gamil –
Foze) bred by Pasha Ahmed Hamza,
Cairo, imported in utero 1971,
Owner: Dr. F. B. Klynstra, Lunteren,
Netherlands
Photograph: H. W. Sylvester*

A horse's eyes are so constructed that they can see much better in the dark than can a rider. The Bedouins have made grateful use of this quality. Horse thieves have trained their horses in special skills for tracking or fleeing through the most different terrain possible.

Lower Jaw

Another breed trait is the greatly developed lower jaw. As a result, the head as seen from above is wedge-shaped. The edge of the semi-circular cheek often stands out beyond the lower profile of the jaw. However, from the molars to the lower jaw, the branches narrow toward the muzzle, so the head seen from the side is again typically wedge-shaped. The strongly-built lower jaw provides an ideal insertion for the powerful chewing muscles, and indicates a well-developed chewing mechanism such as a desert Arabian would need for the hard, tough 'desert grass.'

The jaws' construction lends another typical Arabian characteristic. The two branches of the jawbone widen near the windpipe, much more so than in other breeds. In some Kuhaylans they are 15 cm apart. This allows a greater windpipe diameter, facilitating breathing, and improving the delivery of oxygen. More will be said about this when we discuss the ribcage and the blood.

Nostrils

In Kuhaylans and Saqlawis, the nostrils lie not at the end of the muzzle as in other horse breeds; rather, they are set somewhat higher. The muzzle ends with a probiscus-like, very flexible upper lip. The wings of the nostril end not beside but at the ridge of the muzzle. Desert Arabians' nostrils are long and squared. The inner nostril wing forms a sort of flap so that the finely-haired nostril can be closed in sandstorms, allowing air but not sand through. (*Flade*, 1966). Mu'niqis' nostrils, on the other hand, are not squared at rest; theirs are rounded, such as we see in our own domestic breeds.

When running or excited, the very much widened nostrils flare like trumpets, and stand out from the muzzle. The head almost gives the impression of being made up only of eyes and nostrils.

The Neck

There is a gently curved transition from the head to the neck, followed by a short straight section. The Bedouins call this the "mitbah." It is considered a fault if the crest runs a straight line up to the head.

The length of neck varies by strain. The Kuhaylan has a strong, heavy neck that is somewhat shorter than the Saqlawi's gently curved neck. When excited, the neck is carried very high, making the Arabian look even shorter than it actually is.

The longest necks are seen among the Mu'niqi. The strain name Mu'niqi Hdraji very appropriately means "the family with the longest necks."

Emir Abd-el-Kader wrote, regarding the Arabian's length of neck: "If a horse can drink from a puddle with its legs placed normally, you can be sure that it is perfectly built, and that all other parts of the body are in harmony." The transition from neck to withers shows a slight dip. This, too, is characteristic of the Arabian, like the neck's extraordinary flexibility. Brown called them "snake-like."

The Barrel

A special trait of the Kuhaylan is the well-sprung ribcage. The barrel in cross-section is more or less round, allowing for greater space within the chest cavity. The lungs, accordingly, are relatively larger than for other breeds.

The girth is quite variable among Arabians. The largest is found among the Hamdani; they also have the greatest endurance. The Kuhaylan and the Hadban are almost as good in this respect as the Hamdani. The Saqlawi, however, has less well-sprung ribs, a smaller girth, and less endurance. Even less rounded are relatives of the Muniqi, the Jilfan. However, their chest is very deep, as opposed to the Mukhallad, which is very shallow in the chest, and so stands very high on its legs.

Just as the composition of Arabian bloodlines varies by country in the West, so also do we find significant difference in girth measurements in Arabians from different countries. To detail these differences, I have reduced measurements taken by Flade, Pozo Lora, and myself to a common base height of 15 hh. The number of horses measured is parenthesized:

An eminent characteristic of Arabian
horses: the metallic glint to the coat
*RUALA FEDALA (Golmoud el Ahmar-
Ruala Farida), a Dahman Shawaniah*

Bred by Dr. E. and U. Piduch
Owned by Dabrock Arabians, H. and M.
Schroeder, D-2177 Wingst/W-Germany
Photograph: Dabrock

TABLE:

Mean Values of Arabian Horses' Girth, Figured on a Base of 15 hh.

Egyptian (16)	165 cm
Desert (5)	167 cm
German Egyptian (8)	168 cm
Spanish (96)	172.5 cm
Russian (12)	173.5 cm
East German (16)	178.4 cm
Polish (44)	178.5 cm
German, Marbach (10)	180.0 cm

The variation of girth is not due to the way the foals were raised; rather, they are genetically determined. Breeding Egyptian stallions with mares from the Wuerttemburg State Stud in Marbach clearly showed this. The Egyptian-German get were raised under exactly the same conditions as the other Arabians at Marbach, yet their girth measurements remained much smaller.

The Arabian's depth of girth is somewhat less than half its height at the withers, but here again we see quite consistent differences in the averages by country:

Spain	43.0 % of height (Pozo Lora)
Poland (pre-1929)	43.6 % of height (Flade)
Germany	44.4 % of height (Flade)
Poland (post-1936)	45.0 % of height (Flade)

For breadth of chest, Flade reported:

Poland (pre-1929)	34.6 cm
Spain	38.1 cm (Pozo Lora)
Poland (post 1939)	39.1 cm
Germany	40.0 cm

In these respects, the Arabian purebred is relatively about the same as the European breeds. It has been claimed in the English literature on the topic (*Smythe*, 1957) that the Arabian is so well-ribbed because it has one more rib than other breeds do, i.e., 19 instead of 18. This claim does not coincide with the results of analysing 52 horse skeletons, which show that most Arabians have only 17 pairs of ribs. None were found with 19. Warmbloods generally have 18 pairs of ribs, and only occasionally do they have 17 (*Jones* and *Bogart*, 1971).

The Back

The Arabian's back is exceptionally short. The total length of the barrel is only about 96 % of its height the withers. This short back is a typical breed characteristic. It is regrettable that there are judges today with a definite preference for un-Arabian long backs, especially among stallions. This runs the risk of destroying a typical Arabian breed trait, since breeders, too, often prefer leggy, long-backed stallions.

The Kuhaylan, the Hadban, and the Wadnakhursan have the shortest backs, according to Raswan. The Saqlawi, the Abayyan, and especially the Hamdani are longer in the back. With respect to the length of back, there is hardly any difference among purebred Arabians from different countries. Given as a percentage of height, back lengths were (measured in about 1960):

    in Spain   96.4 %
    in Germany   95.9 %
    in Poland   95.8 %.

The opinion is often found in literature that this short back is due to the Arabian horse having only 5 lumbar vertebrae instead of 6, as in cold- and most warm-blooded horses. (*Osborn*, 1907; *Brown*, 1947,; *Uppenborn*, 1970; *Seydel*, 1933; and *Nissen*, 1964, among others). In fact, many Arabians do have only 5 lumbar vertebrae, but there are also many with 6. The horse mummy found in Egypt and dated from 1490 to 1435 BC had the following vertebrae count: (*Chard*, 1937)

     7 neck vertebrae
    18 thoracic vertebrae
     5 lumbar vertebrae
    14 tail vertebrae

This count of 5 lumbar vertebrae was also found by Professor Osborn, in the American Arabian, NIMR, and by Drahn (1926) in the skelton of a purebred Arabian at the Veterinary College of Berlin. So Arabians were generally considered to have only five lumbar vertebrae and therefore to have a short back.

Jones and Bogart (1971) and Schiele (1972) studied several skeletons and concluded that by far not all Arabians have 5 lumbar vertebrae. According to Schiele, of the 27 Arabians from which data could be obtained, 13 had 5 lumbar vertebrae and 14 of the purebreds had 6. The lumbar vertebrae must not be considered in isolation. Over half a centruy ago, biologists pointed out that the border between thoracic and lumbar vertebrae varies. A vertebrae

NAFTETA (Kaisoon - Moneera) with filly
by Farag:
Hamasa Bint Nafteta, bred and owned by
Olms Arabians Hamasa Stud. Junior
Champion, National Arab Horse Show,
Aachen, 1984, Junior Champion Asil Cup
International, 1985
Photograph: L. Miček, 1st price
Photoexibition Asil Cup Int. 1988

with ribs is called a thoracic vertebra, and one without is a lumbar vertebra. The number of ribs does vary. There are also humans with a few ribs more or less and therefore with a few lumbar vertebrae more or less. In order to draw a conclusion regarding length of back from the number of vertebrae, why not include all back vertebrae, i.e. both thoracic and lumbar? According to statements by Jones and Bogart, 4 of the 7 Arabians they examined had only 17 instead of 18 thoracic vertebrae. As far as I could tell, however, 3 skeletons with 5 lumbar vertebrae had the normal count of 18 thoracic vertebrae.

Following this line of reasoning, it could well be that the Arabian, as a breed, has not one lumbar vertebrae less but rather 23 back vertebrae in comparison to the cold-blood's and the Shetland's 24. A breed characteristic is an attribute shown by the majority of individuals in the breed. But whether or not the number of vertebrae is related to length of back is another question. Humans have 7 neck vertebrae, but so do giraffes, despite their enormously long necks! But then this is comparing two different species. So let us look at dogs, and stay within one species. Here we see breeds with exceptionally long neck i.e. greyhounds, and breeds with short necks, like the mastiff. The number of vertebrae is the same in both cases, i.e., 7.

The Croup

The Arabian was originally slightly overbuilt, i.e., higher at the croup than at the withers. Brown (1947) attributed this to racing. All swift animals derive their driving power from their hindquarters. A somewhat lower forehand was supposed to assist throwing the body forward, he explained. He gave ECLIPSE as an example. This fantastically fast racehorse was also overbuilt. Be that as it may, not all contemporary Europeans Arabians are over-built, as shown in the following table:

TABLE:

Average Height at Whithers and at Croup for European Purebred Arabians after *Flade* and *Pozo Lora* (# horses measured).

Country	Height at Whithers	Height at Croup
Germany (16)	149.6	151.2
Poland (40)	148.4	149.5
Spain (96)	147.6	146.9!

The breadth of hip varies somewhat among Arabians. The narrowest are the Spanish with an average of 43.6 cm, and the widest are the American:

Spain	43.6 cm	(Pozo Lora)
Germany	49.2 cm	(Flade)
Poland	50.2 cm	(Flade)
America	51.1 cm	(Brown)

Stallions are about 2.5 cm broader than mares, while the latter are somewhat lower in the croup (*Brown*).

The pelvis is completely developed in stallions by the age of three, but not until five in mares. This is important for horse breeders. Animals that are not fully mature ought not to be bred. A three year old female horse is still considered a filly. These days, everything must happen as quickly as possible. We cannot expect more. But aren't we over-exploiting our mares, when we breed them as three-year-olds?

The pelvis, zoologists explain, is placed more horizontally in classic Arabians than in cold-bloods and most warm-bloods. The sacral vertebrae above it run slightly upwards. This skeletal structure results in the flat croup with the typical high-set tail. Such conformation is notable in the stallion, IBN MONIET EL NEFOUS. The flat croup is found in the extreme among the Saqlawi. Raswan gives as a distinguishing trait of the Saqlawi that the top-line from withers over the back to the tail is a straight line. This is seen in many Egyptian Arabians.

The Kuhaylan, as a result of their heavier muscling, are of rounder lines. Characteristic for the Muniqi, on the other hand, is a sloping, angular croup with a low-set tail.

Raswan described a further deviation from the straight croup usually thought of as typically Arabian among the Hamdani. Many representatives of this strain have "egg-shaped" hind-quarters.

The Tail

It is usually claimed that the Arabian has fewer tail vertabrae than do other breeds. Osborn said the Arabian has 16 or 17 tail vertebrae; Flade even mentions 15 as opposed to 16 to 20 for other breeds. Schiele collected the results from many experts who in total had examined 25 Arabians. Of these 25, 9 had 18 tail vertebrae. But Schiele reported 18 tail vertebrae for the stallion, NIMR, while the count was 16 according to Osborn (1907). We must say that by far most Arabians have fewer than 18 tail vertebrae. It is interesting that all asil Arabians found to have 5 lumbar vertebrae also had fewer tail vertebrae, i.e., 14 to 17.

As we have seen, the Arabian's tail is set higher than that of other breeds. As a result, the Arabian at rest carries the tail loosely in a gentle curve away from the body. But when excited, the tail carriage is characteristic! Then it is carried vertically, or even draped over the croup. This extreme tail carriage is often seen among the Abayyan. A lovely example is the Abayyah al Majali mare, NIJMEH (see photo p. 54). Notice, too, the typical head carriage and the straightened neck. This is the Arabian in perfection!

It is a regrettable matter that today, even at shows, so many so-called purebred Arabians lack this typical tail carriage. In some cases one may even see tails clamped down on the hindquarters.

Legs

The Arabian's legs, as experts claim, are its greatest advantage. Proof of this lies in the results of the several-day endurance tests in the USA. No other breed has so few disqualifications for lameness or leg injuries as the Arabian. And yet their legs are extraordinarily fine. So fine, indeed, that a spectator at the stallion exhibition in Utrecht asked whether such an Arabian really could carry an adult! The fore cannon's circumference is quite small, in fact, but the cannon bone's construction is extraordinarily tight and solid, and the tendons have been compared to steel. Despite the cannons small circumference, the superficial flexor tendons are remarkably strongly developed.

The leg's coat and the tendon sheath are thin, though, contributing to the drier appearance of the Arabian's leg in comparison to other breeds.

I was able to determine that stallions are less light-boned than mares. One must compare horses of similiar background to demonstrate this, since there is great variation in this regard among the different breeding regions, as seen in the following list:

Germany, stallions (20)	av. 18.1 cm
Germany, mares (20)	av. 17.4 cm
Egypt, stallions (8)	av. 18.3 cm
Egypt, mares (10)	av. 17.0 cm
Spain, mares (15)	av. 17.0 cm
Desert, mares (5)	av. 17.3 cm

As a two-year-old he has already established a highly successfull show record nationally as well as internationally:
K.E.N. ASAM (Masoud-Amal von Mohafez) born 1987
Breeder: C. Jung, Großenkneten
Owner: Katr El Nada Arabian Stud Sylvie Eberhardt, D-6625 Püttlingen-Saar and Dr. H.-J. Nagel, D-2709 Großenkneten

K.E.N. ASAM was Junior Champion at the International Arabian Horse Show and Egyptian Event Europe in Baden-Baden 1989. In the very same year he was named Champion of the pure-bred Arabians at the stallion licensing in Germany and Europe Reserve Junior Champion in Paris.

Russia, mares (10)	av. 18.0 cm
Poland (1899 – 1929, both sexes) (88)	av. 20.0 (Flade)
Trakehner (warmblood)	av. 20.8 (Flade)
Belgian Draft	av. 29.0 (Flade)

The Arabian's cannon is relatively less short than the English Thoroughbred's. Exceptions are the Mu'niqi and the Hamdani, whose cannons are extremely short. The longest cannons are seen among the Milwah. Their knees and hocks really are too high (*Raswan*).

The knee is large, broad, deep, and flat, with an amazingly large joint area. The same is true of the fetlock. Thanks to this structure, the joints can withstand the great concussion of hard footing.

The Coat

One meets here and there in literature the claim that grey is the most frequent color among Arabians in the desert. This is supported with the further claim that this color offers the best camouflage in the desert. But anyone who has been in the Arabic desert lands knows that the modern Arabian army chooses yellow-brown over white as a protective coloring. It may be concluded that white could not be the best camouflage, since the desert is not white, after all.

Doughty also mentions in his book, *Travels in Arabia Deserta* (1888) that not greys but bays were most frequently seen among Arabian horses. Lady Anne Blunt estimates the number of bays among the Anazeh Bedouins horses at 35 %, the dark browns at 20 %, the chestnuts at 15 %, and greys at 30 %. Of course there are great differences between the individual tribes. Thus, Palgrave in 1865 encountered mostly chestnuts and greys in central Arabia. There are also entire strains within the Arabian breed in which grey is never or only rarely found.

According to Raswan, the Hadban strain showed only blood- and dark bays, and the Mu'niqi were always chestnut and bay.

Typically Arabian is the metallic sheen seen in chestnuts as well as bays and greys. Seydel considers this metallic sheen to be almost a sign of a desert Arabian's purity of blood.

A further characteristic is the coat's extraordinary softness. This softness is due to the hair's structure, not its fineness.

TABLE:

Diameter of Hair in 1/1000 mm (Flade: Altenkirch)

Hair	Arabian (5)	Cold-Blood (10)
Front of chest	37	44
Forehead	88	81
Mane	102	94
Tail	182	186

The Arabian's coat is much denser than that of other breeds. On an equal size patch of skin, easily twice as many hairs grow on an Arabian than on a Belgian Draft. While the coat is generally much thicker and the inside of the nostrils and ears are thickly haired, certain parts of the body are very thinly (or not at all) haired. The black skin here shows to the light of day, especially around the eyes, muzzle, and nostrils. Especially for greys, this gives the Arabian a very typical look. This is also the basis for the name Kuhaylan. The black around the eyes reminds one of the eyeshadow (kuhl) many women use.

The Arabian's hair is much shorter than that of other breeds. *Lodemann* (1927) established the following average length of hair taken from the front of the knee.

Belgian Draft	16 mm
Oldenburger	14 mm
English Thoroughbred	11 mm
Arabian	8 mm

Stallions' hair is somewhat longer than mares'.

ANCHOR HILL HALIM
(Hadbah – Silima)
foaled May 5, 1970.
Breeder: Dr. T. E. Atkinson, USA.
Owner: Petra Horsch, Hellmansberg.
An asil champion stallion
from the USA.

Best in Training,
and second place at the
Medingen Stallion
Performance Tests, 1975.
Photograph: Erika Sommer

CHAPTER V

SOME PHYSIOLOGICAL CHARACTERISTICS OF THE BREED

In the desert, feed is extraordinarily scarce for most of the year. The same is true of water. During the rainy season, man and horse can manage well enough, but during dry periods, especially when they are unusually long, the mortality rate among desert inhabitants is high. According to Seydel's data, mortality resulting from deprivation was so great in the 1930's that 50 % of all Arabian foals born and raised in the desert died before reaching the age of four. This is an uncommonly strict natural selection. Only animals capable of exceptional feed utilization reached the age of possibly reproducing themselves. This natural culling has continued for many centuries. The result is a breed of horse of great frugality. For example, I would like to mention the results of an experiment by Flade (1966). In this experiment, five Arabians with an average weight of 1014 pounds were fed such that their weight after 75 days was unchanged. This was achieved on a daily ration of:

	Approx.
Oats	3.31 lb.
Dried Greens	1.10 lb.
Grass Hay, 2nd quality	4.41 lb.
Roots	6.62 lb.
Chaff	2.00 lb.
Straw	2.20 lb.

The carbohydrate value of this ration is 4.41 pounds – only 70% of a light cold-blood's ration figured also on a base weight of 1014 pounds (See *Grashuis*, Table III).

During extremely hard distance rides held in the USA in the 1920's, it was demonstrated that participating Arabians required – almost unbelievably – only 60 % of the feed required by the other participants (Thoroughbred, Quarter Horse, etc.) to win these rides. This proves that the Arabian's feed utilization is better than that of any other saddle horse breed.

Blood

When we run, our breathing rate increases. Our muscles demand more oxygen to combust to meet the higher demand for energy. By breathing faster, more oxygen is taken into the lungs. The blood takes the oxygen from the lungs to the muscles. The blood exchanges oxygen for the carbon dioxide which must be removed after being produced by muscular activity. The faster we run, the faster we breathe, and the faster the blood must circulate to satisfy the muscles' increased demand for oxygen.

In the blood, oxygen is stored in the red corpusles. It is held there by the red pigment, hemoglobin. The more hemoglobin the blood has, the more oxygen it can supply, and the better it can satisfy the muscles' need for oxygen, so the muscles tire less rapidly.

To cover a long distance quickly without exhausting itself too much, an animal must therefore have excellent oxygen delivery system. For the moment, I will disregard the necessary removal of carbon dioxide from the muscles. The same process holds true for it as for the oxygen supply, but in reverse order.

The horse does not differ in this respect from humans. We have already mentioned that Arabians have an especially wide windpipe, so it can more easily and quickly fill the lungs. Due to its barrel-shaped ribcage, the Arabian has room for relatively large lungs. This also helps the oxygen supply. More oxygen is taken in per inhalation. But what use would this more efficient breathing be for the Arabian, if the blood were not able to quickly transport the greater supply of oxygen to the muscles? As shown in experiments by Hansen and Todd (1951), the Arabian has more hemoglobin per liter of blood than other breeds do, so it can move more oxygen per liter of blood.

Average Amount of Hemoglobin (Hb) per Liter of Blood

Cold-blooded stallion	115.1 gram Hb/liter
Warm-blooded stallion	126.7 gram Hb/liter
Arabian stallion	132.0 gram Hb/liter

From *Romijn*, 1948, *Hansen & Todd*, 1951

These values are for the blood's hemoglobin content in horses at rest, however. Nature offers a third means of supplying more oxygen to the muscles when necessary, aside from more rapid breathing and the faster pulse rate. The bone marrow has a very large reserve of red corpusles. Under heavy physical stress, for example in long races, this reserve is sent into the blood. This significantly raises the blood's hemoglobin content, and therefore also raises the capacity to move oxygen from the lungs to the muscles. We could compare it to calling out extra buses during urban rush hours.

Obviously, the total amount of hemoglobin which a horse can supply to the body is of decisive importance to its performance, especially in long-distance rides at high speeds.

Heusser (1952) determined the total amount of hemoglobin a horse can mobilize on a long gallop. He showed that the Arabian horse stands at the top here, too.

Freiberger stallion	178.4 gram Hb/liter
Half-bred stallions	192.8 gram Hb/liter
Arabian stallions	205.2 gram Hb/liter

The Arabian can be considered the standard performance horse, specialized for going long distances in difficult terrain. In the following chapter we shall see that the Arabian is unbeatable over long distances. That its breathing mechanism overshadows that of other breeds has been proven in endurance rides over long distances.

Every year in the western USA, the Tevis Cup 100-Mile-One-Day ride is held. The 100 mile course runs over arid mountains with many almost vertical drops and climbs. The 1972 veterinary data which the organizers kindly made available to me shows that 23 horses covered the distance in nineteen to nineteen and one-half hours. Ten of the 23 horses were purebred Arabians. The time of 19 hours was not the best time; as we shall later see. At the finish, the respiration rates were determined by a veterinarian. On an average, these were:

10 purebred Arabians	29 breaths/minute
13 other horses	34 breaths/minute

Respiration, then, was slower for the Arabians although the horses had relatively 9 more pounds to carry. (An Arabian carried 19.5 % of its own weight, on an average, compared to 18.1 % for other horses).

Fertility

Arabians are very fertile. According to Flade, the number of actual conceptions per 100 breedings was:

Germany	85.4
Poland	77.7

These results vary of course from mare to mare. To illustrate, I have gathered data from ten Arabian mares from the *Weil-Marbach Studbook, 1817 – 1971*. Mares which reached over 20

*MONIET EL NEFOUS OA (Shaloul –
Wanisa). The favorite of General von
Pettkoe-Szandtner, this mare was not only
lovely, she produced outstanding get, and
lived to 30 years of age*

years of age were selected. The number of years in which these mares were bred, how often they remained barren, how frequently they miscarried, and how many living foals they had is shown as follows:

TABLE:
Fertility of Ten Arabian Mares Which Reached the Age of at Least Twenty From the Marbach Stud

Name	Age Reached	Number of Years Bred	Remained Barren	Mis-arried	Foals
Amadine	21	16	3	1	12
Caesarea	23	18	1	2	15
Dinarsad	25	21	7	0	14
Doris	22	13	6	1	6
Isabella	21	16	4	2	10
Jatta	26	21	5	1	15
Sarah	23	18	7		11
Sardine	23	20	2	2	16
Soldateska	24	16	5	0	11
Sylphide	25	20	4	0	16
Average	23.3	18	4.4	0.9	12.6

This Table shows that during their average lifespan of 23 years, the mares were bred in 18 years. From these matings over the 18 years, they remained barren about 4 years, miscarried once on an average, and had an average of 13 living foals.

Before their 20th year, 78 % of the breedings resulted in live foals.

After their 20th year, fertility dropped. Thus, from 33 breedings, the ten aged mares produced:

    15 live foals;

     2 miscarriages; and

    16 matings remained unproductive

In old age, therefore, the percentage of breedings which resulted in birth fell to 48 %.

The foals born to the aged mares could mature to top-grade performance horses, however.

"You shall fly without wings"
The flying gaits of HAMASA KAHILA
(Kaisoon – Shar Zarqa), an outstanding
brood mare who produced 13 foals, at the
age of 18 years. Of her offspring three
stallions were licensed, all of them in the
premium class.
Bred and owned by Olms Arabians
Hamasa Stud, D-6301 Treis/Lda.,
W-Germany

The offspring's vitality is unaffected by the dam age. Well-known examples are Marbach's famous mare, JATTA, and her daughter, SAHMET. JATTA was foaled in 1933 out of the then 22-year-old Arabian mare, SOLDATESKA. At the age of 24, in turn, JATTA gave life to the famous SAHMET, a mare of exceptional beauty which also became a mother to the international champion stallion, SAHER.

One may ask, to what age does an Arabian mare remain fertile? The oldest mare 1 have seen with a foal at foot was a 34-year-old desert Arabian mare in H.R.H. Sharif Nasser ben Jamil's stables in Ruseifa, Jordan. One of the Majali Bedouins' desert mares, the Kubayshah NOFAH, bore a healthy filly foal at the age of 28. Olms saw a 29-year-old mare with a foal at side among the Tahawai Bedouins in 1977. It seems that the desert Arabians may be superior in this regard, too.

Gestation

One often hears that Arabians carry their foals longer than other breeds do.

Nissen (1964) gives the average length of gestation for 'sport horses' as 334 days ± 9.5 days – i.e., gestation for most horses lasts 324.5 to 343.5 days. Adding the various lengths of pregnancy and dividing by the number of pregnancies, we derive the so-called average length of pregnancy, given here as 334 days. I have detailed the term 'average pregnancy' here because I have so often been asked, "How is it that my mare is a week overdue? Should I call in the vet?"

The length of pregnancy depends on many factors, such as the mare's inclinations, as well as feed, work, and climate. Also, the gestation is on an average somewhat longer for colt foals, by about 1-1/2 days than for filly foals.

For Arabians, the literature reporting gestation varies, and differs from country to country:

Spain	343 days	(Pozo Lora)
Iran	341 days	(Baumeister)
Hungary	339.3 days	(Lehndorff)
Germany	338 days	(Baumeister)

These scores are actually a bit higher than the average length of pregnancy given by Nissen. However, if we compare the averages within one country – Germany, for example – we see the following picture:

Arabian	338.0 days	(Baumeister)
Heavy warmblood	338.4 days	(Flade)
Mecklenburger	339.9 days	(Flade)
Trakhener	336.8 days	

Thus, it cannot be flatly claimed that Arabian mares carry their foals longer than other breeds do theirs.

Life Expectancy

How old does an Arabian live to be? It is well-known that Arabians are long-lived. We often see Arabians far above 20 years old. Who in Holland does not know of the elderly SAOUD? Foaled in 1946 and still spritely at 28. And RUDAN? In his mid-20's he was still an excellent breeding stallion. At Ruseifa in Jordan, I saw, as just mentioned, a 34-year-old mare with her foal. The 30-year-old MONIET EL NEFOUS stood at El Zahraa until just recently, a beauty to the last. The Egyptian stallion, ANTER, was 26 years old when he passed on in 1972. The list goes on. Everyone probably knows of Arabians who have reached a very old age, so we tend to be quick to say, yes, an Arabian will easily live to 30 and beyond.

What is the average lifespan achieved by Arabians? Comfort (1962) researched 189 Arabian mares in the *Annex to the General Stud Book*. These 189 English Arabians had an average lifespan of 18.8 years.

On an average, therefore, the Arabian in England reached an age of almost 19 years. The English Thoroughbred had a lower average life expectancy of 17 years, in England.

In German and Egyptian studbooks, I have reviewed the average life expectancy of horses from Marbach and from El Zahraa.

At El Zahraa between 1966 and 1970, 37 adult horses and 20 young foals died. Because Comfort disregarded foal mortality, I will do so also, since the average lifespans would otherwise not be comparable. The average age of the 37 Egyptian Arabians was 15. Only 7 died after having reached 20 years of age. The oldest, HAMDAN (IBN RABDAN x BINT RADIA), reached the age of 31. Seven others had not reached 10 years of age.

In the Weil-Marbach studbook, the dates of death of 22 Arabian mares are given. They reached an average age of 17.6 years. Seven of the 22 mares had to be put down because of advanced heaves caused by the unfavorable cold and humid climate. Two had died in labor and one died of colic.

The foal mortality rate in Marbach between 1940 – 1970 stood at eight animals out of 143 births.

TABLE:

Average Life Expectancy of the Purebred Arabian

Egypt, El Zahraa (37)	14.9 years
Germany, Marbach (22)	17.6 years
England (189)	18.9 years

It is truly remarkable that in El Zahraa, despite a climate so favorable to Arabians – warm and dry – and despite the excellent veterinarian care, the life expectancy is so low. Is beauty too great a concern there, to the neglect of vitality?

The high carriage of the tail is another major characteristic of the asil Arabian. The picture shows the brilliant bay stallion A.K. BAY MONIET (Ibn Moniet el Nefous – Shallha)

Bred by Bentwood Farm Owned by Bill and Shirley Reilich, Alpharetta, Georgia 30201/USA

CHAPTER VI

ABOUT THE TEMPERAMENT

Antonius' categorization of the domestic horse into three type-groups: Equus orientalis; Equus ferus; and, Equus robustus, is an unsuitable method of categorizing horse behavior. For his investigations, Zeeb (1955) chose Speed-Eberhardt's four prototypes of horse behaviour in its relationship to humans:

Prototype I: exists in almost pure form in the Exmoor Pony;

Prototype II: existed in almost pure form in the extinct Devon packhorse. It was recorded as of 6000 B.C. in England and on the Continent;

Prototype III: large stature, tall; trunk long and narrow. Head long, narrow, roman-nosed, and pig-eyed. Much less specialized than Types I and II. Traces of blood recognizable in cold-bloods.

Prototype IV: Small stature, delicate, short backed. Head narrow and short with a concave profile. Parrot-mouthed, browses rather than grazes. Finds in North Germany. Formerly probably in sub-tropical times and in regions of Europe. Blood remains in Arabian as well as Libyan, Persian, and similar breeds – *Haltennorth*, 1955

Although he did not pursue their significance as possible prime models, Dr. Klaus Zeeb (1958) was able to recognize four types of behavior in the models of horses he reviewed. Certain models of appearance consistantly showed certain models of behavior as well. We must be careful, though, when trying to attribute the behavior model of Prototype IV to our purebred Arabians! Zeeb described horses of extreme Prototype IV appearance, as opposed to pure Arabians, as being easily excitable and inclined toward kicking. So we are looking at a basic difference between pure (asil) Arabians and mixed-breeds with an Arabian appearance – a hint for us to take temperament into account when selecting breeding stock. In this respect it is interesting to quote Raswan/Guttman: *"The knowledgeable breeder also has the most reliable horse, since the purer an Arabian is, the more kind and harmonious it reveals its temperment to be. Here lies the secret already much speculated upon in the West."* Temperment is determined not only genetically. Environment also plays a role. A horse born and raised in the desert which spent its youth in and around the black

Le Derviche.

carle Vernet

80

tents in the Bedouins' camps will certainly have quite a different character than its counterpart raised on a European stud farm. A horse ridden by a daredevil Bedouin will also behave differently than one with a timid rider in the saddle.

The desert Arabian's reliability, courage, good character, and high intelligence are generally recognized. One could almost say that they are breed traits. I would like to illustrate the Arabian horse's nature with a few examples. NIJMEH showed me how courageous a desert mare could be. One evening, we were trotting along the edge of some woods. I was riding her with neither curb nor snaffle, just a simple halter. The sun had set and it was already rather dark when we came upon some soldiers. An entire troop in camouflage was en route to night exercises. As I rode by them at a walk, they suddenly began to shout and clap. NIJMEH pranced in excitement. The soldiers' stupid and, for some riders, dangerous behavior irritated me, and I wanted to speak to the infantrymen about it. Mocking laughter was the answer. I turned to find the sergeant. Being upset, my aids were probably too rough. NIJMEH misunderstood, and thought I wanted to attack the soldiers. She plunged toward the men at a gallop, jumped in the middle of the group, and whirled about. Some soldiers fell, others threw themselves under cover, and rifles clattered to the ground, as NIJMEH fled. Fifty yards down the road we turned to see the astonished soldiers regaining their feet and sheepishly gathering up their weapons. Luckily no one had been hurt by the courageous little mare's attack.

Rollo Springfield relates: *"One of the most signal instances of courage on the part of horse and rider, and of perfect concert between both, is that recorded of the late Sir Robert Gillespie and his Arab. Sir Robert being present on the race course of Calcutta during one of the great Hindoo festivals, where many thousands are assembled to witness all sorts of shows, was suddenly alarmed by the shrieks and commotion of the crowd. On being informed that a tiger had escaped from his keepers, he immediately called for his horse, and, with no other weapon than a boar spear snatched from one of the by-standers he rode to attack this formidable enemy. The tiger was probably amazed at finding himself in the middle of such a number of shrieking beings flying from him in all directions; but the moment he perceived Sir Robert, he crouched in the attitude of preparing to spring upon him; at that instant the gallant soldier passed his horse in a leap over the tigers back, and struck the spear through his spine. It was a feat requiring the utmost conceivable unity of purpose on the part of horse and rider, almost realizing for a moment the fable of the centaur. Had either swerved or wavered for a moment, both had been lost. But the brave steed knew his rider. The animal was a small grey and was afterwards sent home as a present to the Prince Regent."* (Springfield, 1874).

HAMASA ZARIF
(Farag OA – Shar Zarqa).
An endearing personality even
as a foal, an alert little fellow,
and beautiful as well.
Owner: Dr. F. B. Klynstra

The Arabians natural confidence in man, coupled with centuries of training no doubt accounts a little for the innate courage of the Arabian. The stallion ABU ZEYD was never sufficiently disturbed to retreat from a whistling or steaming locomotive, or a Fourth of July parade, even if fire-crackers were exploding beneath his feet, although sweat would roll off him and he would tremble beneath his rider.

Fortitude is as marked a virtue in an Arabian as courage. It has been noted on the tracks of the East that the Arabian, even though fired and blistered on both legs at once, and undoubtedly in great pain, will not refuse his nose bag. Sick or injured horses often endure considerable pain inflicted by human attempts to relieve their sufferings. (Brown, 1929).

Walter G. Olms experienced such a case at his Hamasa Stud Farm in Treis with the MORAFIC son, FARAG. One day, when standing up after rolling, FARAG caught his hoof between the oak door's sharp corner and the cement wall, because a groom had neglected to close the stall's lower latch. Trapped, FARAG initially made a few attempts to free himself, but he could not extricate his leg. He neighed and remained calm until he was released from this dangerous situation, which would have panicked most other horses and thus cost them their lives. From the hock down, the leg looked very bad and was bleeding profusely. The vet came to treat him, but FARAG would not let him near until Walter Olms himself arrived. Olms sent everyone out, saying that he would have to explain the situation to FARAG first. He spoke quietly and calmly to FARAG for a moment, and then called the vet back in. FARAG stood like a rock.

FARAG's stud colt, HAMASA ZARIF, performed the following act shortly thereafter when he was 10 months old. He had curiously stuck his head through a 3-yard-wide gate and slipped, getting stuck in the framing in the middle. He lifted the gate off the hinges, since there was no other way to free himself. With the gate frame right and left of him like bi-plane wings, he cantered about the yard, amazed and a bit annoyed. No one dared to approach him; they ducked for cover as the horse-airplane approached. Finally he discovered the open way to the arena and proceeded at a lovely working canter through the door with the almost hundred-pound frame swinging from his neck. Everyone held their breath, since a bump on the side would surely have thrown him down and broken his neck. As if that were not enough the next doors were also open: to the arena, out of the arena, and also to the first pasture. They all ran after him, but HAMASA ZARIF, who otherwise was always one to dash through the gates close to the post, cantered tamely through the middle of the second, third, and fourth gates. Once in the downhill sloping pasture, he braked to a stop and shook the gate loose with one jerk. Without a scratch, he trotted proudly back to the arena.

The following experience is less believable. I would not have believed it, had I not seen it with my own eyes. HAMASA ZARIF came to my farms a yearling, where upon he befriended one of our dogs, Pomka. He became almost obsessed with playing with her. As she teased him one day from the other side of the fence, he lifted Pomka – who weighed over eighty pounds over the three and a half foot fence by grabbing her by the loose skin on her neck. Even my wife didn't believe me, until two weeks later when she saw the same thing. She also saw the dog – a very sharp Belgian Bouvier de Flanders, a type of heavy, large Schnauzer – lick ZARIF sweetly on the nose as he gently lowered her to the ground.

Both of these experiences make believable the stories of war mares carrying their injured masters from the battlefield. (See Mazoilleier in Daumas, *Horses of the Sahara*).

"… *Of the horses, the Arabian is the most intelligent, and has certain functions of the mind highly developed, such as memory, fortitude, and docility, that makes him an extremely useful servant of man; and because he possesses the rudiments of many other mental functions, he is a most interesting companion.*" (*Brown*, 1929).

In respect to Arabian horses, one may speak of a certain intelligence. Intelligence is the ability to grasp a situation immediately and to react to it. NIJMEH gave me a lovely example of this. She had injured her hind leg badly one day. My wife treated the wound daily with ointment. Since infection can easily set in around stables, NIJMEH was allowed to relax at pasture in the sun and breeze. At first, someone held her while my wife treated the wound. After a few days, though, NIJMEH would come up to the fence herself as soon as my wife showed her the jar of ointment. Then she would stand in front of my wife and raise the injured leg to be treated.

One of the most excellent Asil Arabian stallions bred in Europe:
Three times National Supreme Champion of South Africa and in 1988 in addition winner of the riding class:
HAMASA EL FAGR (Farag – Menha)

Bred by Olms Arabians Hamasa Stud
Owned by Johrhemar Dr. van Wyk, ZA-Klerksdorp/South Africa
Photograph: I. L. Viloen

SATURF (Fa-Turf – Sagitta), grey stallion foaled 1966. A grandson of the outstanding TURFA and the famous FADL. Like his grandsire, successful in distance rides, Working Cow Horse, and Western Pleasure competitions, and winner of the 1974 Levi Ride and Tie Race in Goodwell, Oklahoma. Breeder and owner: M. Mayo. Beaver, Oklahoma.

CHAPTER VII

ENDURANCE

In the West, the Arabian is often considered little more than a lovely show horse. Some see the breed as an 'ornament', and to them, breeding Arabians is an expensive hobby for the rich. Many purebred Arabians die never having carried a rider. They are spoiled and pampered like fragile lap dogs. Stables with central heating or stalls with electric heaters are fortunately still the exception. But that these exist at all is regrettable. Such aberations make the Arabian laughable in the eyes of other horsemen, which in no way is deserved by these noble horses.

The Arabian is a high-performance horse like none other. It can survive where any other horse would die in misery. For many, many centuries, it has been able to thrive amid the tremendous hardships of desert life – burning heat and bitterest cold, dryness, severe thirst, and rainstorms and snowstorms.

The mountains of northern Arabia are no strangers to snow. The horses bear this all in the wide open spaces. Nomads such as the Bedouin know no stables. Despite the fact that their horses are mercilessly exposed to the elements, broken wind is unknown among desert Arabians. Animals that were not resistant enough died as foals and so could not propagate themselves. This natural culling process is totally lacking in our countries. The only way we can tap into this natural selection process is to import these hardened desert horses. I refer above all to stallions intended for stud. Our famous expert on animal husbandry and genetics, Dr. A. L. Hagendoorn, has already pointed this out in his book, *Animal Breeding*. The Arabian purebred was especially referred to in this regard. But to return to the Arabian's ability to perform – I will go into greater detail regarding his ability as a race horse in a later chapter. Here, I would like to praise his endurance and recuperative powers. No other breed of horse can compare to the Arabian in this regard, not earlier and not now. Arabians are still on top for long-distance rides. What they have achieved in this field borders on the unbelieveable.

In August of 1929, in the scorched Arabian desert about 180 miles from Kuwait, 512 Bedouins of the Mutayr tribe rode to the well of Um Ar-Ruthuma to quench their thirst. Unfortunately, they encountered a stronger force of Shammar Bedouins there. The Mutayr prince, Azaiyiz, was shot from his horse during the battle, and his troops were eventually cut down. One of his men managed to catch the sheikh's mare and flee. The mare was a thirteen-year-old bay Saqlawiyah-Jidraniyah called ANJAYMAH. The Bedouin and ANJAYMAH covered the 180 miles back to Kuwait in three days. There were no wells along the route, so neither horse nor rider had a drop of water for three days of 120°F temperatures. Horse and rider both survived the trip, but it took the mare months to recuperate. This story was recorded by the English colnel, H.R.P. Dickson, who then was living in Kuwait. ANJAYMAH is pictured in the *Raswan Index*, 2nd edition, Part III, photo 98. (See also J. H. Miller, *Verrat in schwarzen Zelten*, 1977, p. 159).

Desert Arabians are still capable today of such extraordinary feats. This I gathered during a conversation with H.R.H. Sharif Nasser ben Jamil during my visit to his stud farm in Ruseifa, Jordan. We stood before an old, very noble mare with a black marking on her hip. It was WAHIDA, once the favorite of King Faisal of Iraq, another member of the Hashemite princely house and nephew of Sharif Nasser. In 1958, King Faisal and his entire family were murdered by revolutionaries. His horses were auctioned publicly by those then in power. Sharif Nasser reported that, "I tried to buy WAHIDA, since I wanted to keep this old bloodline in our family. This was not allowed. Anyone could buy her, provided she never returned to the stables of a member of the Hashemite Royal house. I simply didn't accept that. I remembered that we have in Jordan a very bold horse thief whom I had sent to Iraq. He had a black stallion which he trained especially to be ridden in the darkest night over the most difficult terrain. The usual desert routes would of cause have to be avoided. They rested by day in some den, and rode on by night."

Their route led them through the most isolated stretches – those which everyone else avoided. There were only five wells in a distance of 372 miles. The daring attempt was successful. WAHIDA was rescued from the upstarts before she fell into unknown hands to be lost forever for breeding. During the flight back to Jordan, the stallion died of thirst and exhaustion. WAHIDA, though, came back to the stud farm in good health, and thereafter gave life to many foals. A murderous ride of 745 miles through the most isolated desert saved a valuable old bloodline from extinction.

I could recount many exceptional deeds done by Arabian horses in their native land; most of them rely on oral reports. For Western Europeans, though, perhaps the more sober accounts of the well-organized distance rides in America are more valuable. Horses of various breeds have and still do take part in these competitions, so we can also derive some comparisons.

*100 miles
in one day*

*The course
covers
indescribably
difficult terrain*

The first distance ride in the USA in which Arabians took part was in Vermont on September 18 and 17, 1913. The ride covered a very long distance, and only time counted. It must have been a sight! One hundred fifty-four miles carrying a weight of 160 lbs! The winner was the asil Arabian, YAOUIS, a 13-year-old grey stallion, a Kuhaylan-Ajuz. He ran the 154 miles in 30 hours and 16 minutes.

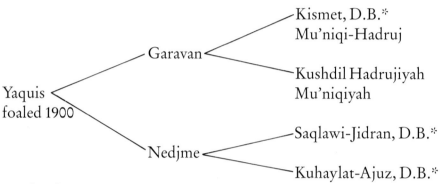

Yaquis
foaled 1900

Garavan

Kismet, D.B.*
Mu'niqi-Hadruj

Kushdil Hadrujiyah
Mu'niqiyah

Nedjme

Saqlawi-Jidran, D.B.*

Kuhaylat-Ajuz, D.B.*

*D.B. = desert-bred

The purebred Arabian stallion, RODAN, a 7-year-old, finished four minutes behind YAQUIS. RODAN was imported in utero from Crabbet park, England, in 1906, and was also a Kuhaylan-Ajuz.

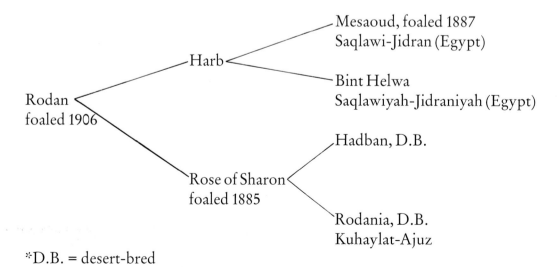

Rodan
foaled 1906

Harb

Mesaoud, foaled 1887
Saqlawi-Jidran (Egypt)

Bint Helwa
Saqlawiyah-Jidraniyah (Egypt)

Rose of Sharon
foaled 1885

Hadban, D.B.

Rodania, D.B.
Kuhaylat-Ajuz

*D.B. = desert-bred

It may be of interest to many that we meet RODAN's grandparents in many English and Dutch Arabians' pedigrees.

To determine which breed was best suited to long-distance rides under heavy weight, 5 distance rides were held in the USA between 1919 and 1925. The first was held October 14-18, 1919. Sixty miles were to be covered for five consecutive days, carrying 200 pounds. The highest score that could be achieved was 100 points, thusly:

    25 points for speed

    25 points for feed utilization

    50 points for condition

The winner was the 10-year-old asil Arabian mare, RAMLA, in 51 hours and 26 minutes for the total distance of 300 miles. RAMLA, foaled in 1909, was Kuhaylat-Ajuz from Crabbet Park, England. She, too, was a granddaughter of Mesaoud and Rose of Sharon.

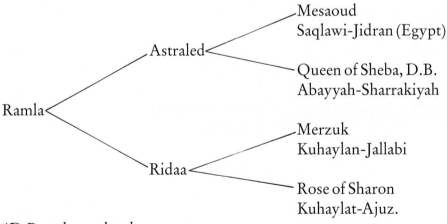

Ramla
- Astraled
  - Mesaoud
    Saqlawi-Jidran (Egypt)
  - Queen of Sheba, D.B.
    Abayyah-Sharrakiyah
- Ridaa
  - Merzuk
    Kuhaylan-Jallabi
  - Rose of Sharon
    Kuhaylat-Ajuz.

*D.B. = desert-bred

By far the most difficult test was the third one, held in October, 1921. Two hundred forty-five pounds were to be carried! Again, the route was five 60-mile stretches marked out by the army. Long stretches over macadam street were included intentionally. The hard pavement posed the greatest demands on the horses' legs, making it quickly clear which breed had the soundest legs. The owners of the English Thoroughbreds gave their all to win this test. In the first spring months, 16 promising Thoroughbreds were carefully selected for training. After completing their training, 8 of best were entered in this distance ride. In all, 17 horses competed. The ride proved to be so difficult that, despite intensive training, only seven horses finished. The winer was again an asil Arabian, the 12-year-old CRABBET, a Kuhaylan Dejani, line-bred to MESAOUD and bred at Crabbet Park, England. Prior to this victory, the chestnut stallion had already posted a sensational success in 1920 by setting the record for 57 miles – 8 hours and 19 minutes, carrying 245 pounds!

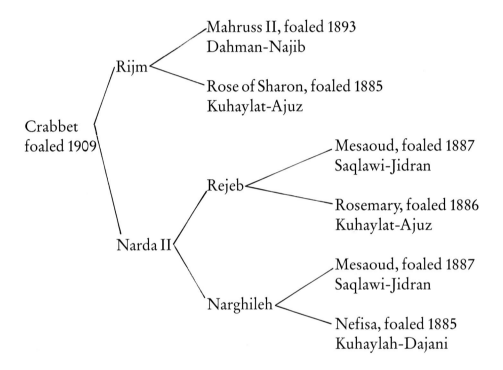

Crabbet
foaled 1909

Rijm
Mahruss II, foaled 1893
Dahman-Najib

Rose of Sharon, foaled 1885
Kuhaylat-Ajuz

Narda II

Rejeb
Mesaoud, foaled 1887
Saqlawi-Jidran

Rosemary, foaled 1886
Kuhaylat-Ajuz

Narghileh
Mesaoud, foaled 1887
Saqlawi-Jidran

Nefisa, foaled 1885
Kuhaylah-Dajani

A still faster time was posted in the summer of 1935 in Holland by the Arabian stallion, AKAL (owned by Dr. C. R. von Vloten). Ridden by Mr. Barlagen, he galloped 37 miles during a heat wave in 90°F temperatures. The start was at the Stadskanaal. The first phase was 20.5 miles at a canter, no walking or trotting. In Borger, he was allqwed a few minutes rest. AKAL drank one small bucket of water, and his temperature was taken – 102.5°F. The second phase was 7.5 miles, also covered at a canter. AKAL's temperature now was 101.5°F. After a ten-minute pause, he galloped on. The last 9 miles led back to the Stadskanaal. AKAL's temperature as taken at the finish was the same as at the start! The total time including pauses was 3 hours and 42 minutes.

Back in his stall, AKAL rolled comfortably and ate his evening oats as if nothing had happened. Professor Van der Plank and some veterinary students from Utrecht had supervised the ride from an accompanying car.

Who was AKAL? He was an Abayyan-Sharrak bred in Sussex, England, foaled in 1928 out of ALMAS (a great-granddaughter of MESAOUD) by SHELOOK. It is interesting to note that SHELOOK is linebred to the desert-bred MOOTRUB, who had a successful racing career in India.

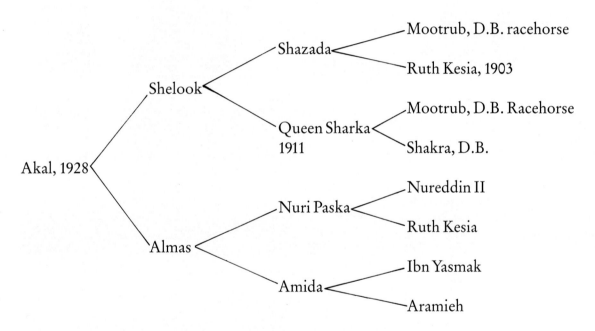

Not just in days past have tough, little Arabians brought off such feats. No, they still do today, especially in the USA. In the *Arabian Horse World*, May 1969, I read an article titled, "Arabians Sweep Florida 18th Annual 100-Mile Competitive Endurance Ride." It reported the decisive victory of five purebred Arabians and one half-Arab. These six won 1st, 2nd, and 3rd places in both the light – and heavyweight divisions of the 18th 100-Mile endurance ride in Florida. This three day ride was held in March, 1968. The Arabians were far superior to the Mustangs, Appaloosas, Quarter Horses, etc. Among the winning Arabians, two were sons of NIZZAM from Dr. Houtappel's stud farm in Rodania, Holland – PAZZAM and GEYMINI CRICKET.

In the US, about ten 100-mile distance rides are organized annually, which always generate great interest. The most difficult of all is probably the Western States Trail Ride (Tevis Cup) through the Sierra Nevadas in California. I would like to close this short overview with a report on this 100-mile endurance race.

It is Saturday, August 7, 1971. We are in Tahoe City on the western flanks of the Sierra Divide in California. The moon is full. At 4:45 A.M., they'll mount up. At 5:00 A.M. sharp, the 150 participants in the Western States Trail Ride will start. The original number of entries was substantially higher, but the thorough vet examination has eliminated a few dozen.

Numerous officials led the riders to the start, seven miles away at the Papoose Parking Lot. Here, they are divided into groups of ten and started at two minute intervals. The first groups departed under the moonlight, but the sun was well above the Sierra Divide's snow-covered peaks by the time the last groups began the 2700 ft. climb up Emigrant Pass.

We are now 7900 feet above sea-level. The ride leads on over stony crags, past grassy mountain meadows, and through pine forests to Robinson's Flats, about 26 miles to the east.

Donna Fitzgerald, on her 9-year-old purebred Arabian gelding, WITEZARIF, is the first to reach the control post. Last year this pair won the coveted first prize, the Tevis Cup. Can they do it again? It is exactly 9:34 A.M. She has a led of only two minutes over Kathy Thomas on her 9-year-old purebred Arabian mare, DYNAMITE. WITEZARIF's pulse is 60 beats per minute upon arrival, and drops to 56 within half an hour; his respiration falls from 28 to 20 per minute during this required rest period. Kathy has already asked too much of her mare, DYNAMITE; she has run her beyond the mare's strength. Upon arrival, her pulse is 160, respiration 52. Just within the prescribed time, the pulse is back down to 70. It doesn't look too rosy, being so close to the limit. A pulse over 70 would have disqualified her. Norman Brostad with his Arabian, FERIAR, is disqualified from further competition for this reason. In all, six were eliminated.

The horses have covered 33 miles. The most difficult phase is yet to come. At first it runs leisurely through luxurious mountain forests to the Last Chance mine. Then... a very steep downhill ride to the floor of the 2600 foot deep American River Canyon, and then through the almost impassably violent river torrents with a steep climb on the other bank. The stony path is hardly rideable, having been cut with dynamite by Gold Rushers in the 1850's, and is in the same condition today as then: Above, on the canyon rim, many riders dismount and run down the cliff-face leading their horses. The temperature here is every bit of 100°F: Through the cold water and up the canyon. Some have their horses pull them up, hanging

*The 100 mile distance
was not too much for the
23-year-old mare AMINA,
difficult though the terrain
may have been*

on their tails! They trot through the once-booming gold prospectors' town of Deadwood. Abandoned now, its only residents lie in the graveyard. The third official halt: Devil's Thumb. Donna Fitzgerald on her Arabian is still in first place, arriving at 12:44. Pulse – 80, respiration – 76. Good! Thirteen minutes later, Elwin Wines follows on MEMSAHIB, a 7-year-old Arabian. Pulse – 88, respiration – 112! (60/36 after 30 minutes). In third and fourth places are Sam Sewald and Marion Robie's Arabians. Sam's DON PABLO is carrying 221 pounds, while Donna's carrying 'only' 185 pounds. Kathy Thomas must take it a little slower now. She is in sixth place, about one hour behind.

After Devil's Thumb comes the very deep Eldorado Canyon. Imagine: down a 3000 foot steep, stony cliff face, and then 2290 feet up, in a temperature of 104°F.

At the Michigan Bluff control station, 94 of the 150 entries are still in the running. Sam Seward despite carrying 221 pounds, has overtaken Marion Robie and is now in 3rd place behind Donna Fitzgerald and Elwin Wines.

Four Arabians in the lead! Forty miles to go, with only a small time difference between the four.

Donna and Elwin pick up the tempo. The terrain is getting easier. There are still a few slopes and a canyon to negotiate. Marion also speeds up. They reach Echo Hills. Donna is still in the lead. Elwin follows, 13 minutes behind. Marion has passed Sam and is now in third place.

Donna's gelding's pulse is 84, respiration 80, upon arrival. After a 30-minute rest, his pulse is down to 68 and respiration down to 40. Marion Robie's Arabian, KOKO, had 84/56 upon arrival, and 52/40 when departing and is therefore less tired. Does she still have a chance? They ride on! Only 15 miles to go! No, Donna stays in the lead and gallops through the finish line in Auburn at 9:24 PM. Applause! She wins the Tevis Cup for the second time. She covered 100 miles in 12 hours and 35 minutes. Among the 15 horses that placed, 11 (!) were purebred Arabian. The first Thoroughbred was 37th, with a time of 19 hours and 21 minutes.

The Arabian mare, AMINA, has not been mentioned yet. At 21 years of age, she finished the ride, and did it again the next year within the prescribed time and in excellent condition. Only an Arabian could manage that.

The following time plan is given to elucidate:

10 minutes walk = .6 miles (100 m/min.)
10 minutes trot = 1.4 miles (220 m/min.)
8 minutes canter = 2.0 miles (400 m/min.)

Thus, 4 miles are covered in 28 minutes; repeated 25 times, 100 miles are covered in 11 hours and 40 minutes. That means 50 miles at a canter (!), 34.5 miles at a trot, and 15.5 miles at a walk. An additional difficulty in the Tevis Cup ride is the 9350 foot height to be climbed and the total 15,600 foot very steep, almost impassable drops along stony paths.

Looking at the results of this extremely difficult long-distance ride, it is clear that no single breed of horse can beat the Arabian in quickly covering great distances under heavy loads, regardless of what fans of other breeds may claim. Consider, too, that the average height of Arabians participating in American endurance rides is not quite 15 hh, and their average weight is only 860 pounds. (For the English Thoroughbred, the respective statistics were 16 hh and 1023 pounds.)

As we recall, the Arabians in these tests were carrying 245 pounds (October, 1921) and were in top condition. The secret of their success doubtless lies in their short back. It is very regrettable to see more and more purebred Arabians with much too long backs! A typical and extremely important Arabian breed characteristic threatens to be lost through incorrect selection of breeding stock.

He won the long-distance driving over 90 kms:
National Champion 1989
HAMASA GHARBI (Gharib-Hamasa Tumaderah)
The day after the victory in the federal
Championship: Hamasa Gharbi is fresh as
the morning dew again.
Bred by Olms Arabians Hamasa Stud,
D-6301 Treis/Lda./W-Germany
Owned by H. Werner Falk,
D-2905 Portsloge/W-Germany

CHAPTER VIII

RACING ARABIANS AND ARABIAN HORSERACING

It was not so long ago that Arabian purebreds were simply registered as a matter of course in the racehorse breed (i.e., Thoroughbred) studbooks in some countries. In England, the Arabian did not have its own studbook until 1919. Prior to that, they were registered in the *General Stud Book*. The reason for this was that the English Thoroughbred is a hybrid, with a large percentage of Arabian blood. Even during the reign of Charles II (1660 – 1683), Arabian horses were imported to England. These horses are considered the ancestors of the English Thoroughbred.

The actual foundation sires came from the Near East: the BYERLY TURK, the GODOLPHIN ARABIAN, and the DARLEY ARABIAN. It is therefore understandable that from time to time Thoroughbred breeders have relied on Arabian stallions to improve the breed. One of these breeders was the famous Sir Wilfred Scawen Blunt, patron of the so famous Crabbet Arabian Stud in Sussex, England. In an article titled *"The Forthcoming Arab Race in Newmarket,"* appearing in the magazine, *Wallace's Monthly,* Blunt wrote:

"About four years ago it was permitted to me to sketch in the pages of this Review, my ideas about the Arabian as a thoroughbred horse, and to call attention to the advantage it might be to English breeders to acquire a fresh strain of pure blood in addition to that already possessed by them. I argued that, the functions of the thoroughbred being twofold – namely, those of a racehorse and of a sire for halfbred stock – the existing English horse could not be relied on as fulfilling either duty in an entirely satisfactory manner. As a racehorse he was degenerating in stoutness if not in speed; and as a sire he had acquired certain faults of constitution and tempo which, while leaving him the best we had, made him no longer the best we could aspire to have. I contrasted him with the Arabian on both these points and to the Arabians advantage."

On the basis of this reasoning, Blunt imported fast Arabians and tried to breed them larger, to defeat the English Thoroughbred on the racetrack. Initially he appeared to have some

FADL OA (Ibn Rabdan – Mahroussa), bred in 1930 by Prince Mohammed Ali, imported to the USA by Henry Babson. A son of the most typey stallion of his day, out of the fantastically lovely top mare, MAHROUSSA. FADL was many times a champion in distance rides, was an outstanding polo pony, and became the most successful breeding stallion of his days in the USA.

success. *A. B. Allen* wrote about this in an article, *"Arab Horses"* which also appeared in *Wallace Monthly* (1875 – 1893):

"We learn that Sir Wilfred has been quite successful in his efforts, and that the prospect is that the third generation will equal in size, power, and speed a good average of the English thoroughbred; be entirely free of any of his inherent diseases and vices of temper; more gentle and courageous, and perhaps prove more hardy and lasting. If Sir Wilfred accomplishes all this, he will then have stallions which will be highly beneficial to breed, to choice thoroughbred mares, resulting in an improvement, to a certain extent, though not in speed of shortraces, of their offspring."

Blunts choice of Arabians were therefore not Show-Horses of the ideal Arabian type but speedy, stout and powerful horses as showed by Peter Upton 'Stammpferde der Araberzucht', 1980.

he average mean of the Kaliber Index of these desertbred stallions (5) was 149,2. Egyptian stallions (8) imported in Germany show an average Kaliber Index 131.

As we now know, however, Wilfrid Blunt's experiment failed. Yet, admiration for the Arabian's racing ability was clearly recognized even decades later. This is shown in the *Arab Horse Studbook*, Vol. I, published in 1919, as well as other places. We find horses which had successful racing careers behind them in India or Egypt, but for which the parentage, strain, breeder or often even the age were completely unknown. One of these Arabian racehorses was the stallion, CROSBIE. The data entered for this horse registered as an Arabian in England in the *Arab Horse Studbook*, Vol. I, p. 36, are inadequate:

"CROSBIE, 1908, Grey. Foaled in the Arabian Desert, and brought to Abassia, where he was purchased by the present owner. Winner of many prizes at shows. Winner of races, Municipal Cup, Alexandria, 1913."

Further down, the stallion, ZOOWAR, is entered, whose age is not even known: *"ZOOWAR. Aged (how aged? – Aut.) Grey. A purebred Arab, bred in Arabia, imported from India by Major Ollivant, Xllth Royal Lancers. A winner of races in India. Winner of prizes."*

Any further information about these horses is unknown. They were excellent racing Arabians, but would they be considered truly purebred Arabians under the circumstances today?

That Arabians can be good racehorses is evidenced by the great popularity of horse racing in the Arabic world since ages past. Aly Mazaheri (1969) described Muslim life during the Middle Ages, saying:

"Horse racing, too, was very popular, and many spectators laid bets on certain horses. The greatest impression was made by the race course at Samarra, which has now been unearthed by archeologists. It lies outside the city, and is about seven miles long, and the excellent track is oval."

The distances run in those days were apparently a good deal longer than we are accustomed to today.

As the Emir Abd el Kader, the great Arabian prince, explained early in the past century, horse racing in Arabia can be traced back to long before Mohammed, i.e., before the 7th century A.D. These races remained unchanged until the 19th century, he continues. This follows from the words of the Prophet, who once said that *"the Angels watch over only three of man's pleasures: the practice of war, the husband's enjoyment of his wife, and horse racing."*

As Mohammed spoke these words in 612, horse racing must truly have been very much in fashion.

But horse racing in those days differed considerably from that to which we are accustomed. According to Abd el Kader, Mohammed recommended about seven miles for trained horses. The number of entries was also prescribed: no more and no less than ten. The seven fastest were richly celebrated in a large tent. Each received a prize. The last three were simply upbraided publicly. There was no betting, since Mohammed had strictly forbidden betting on horses.

Later, in the larger cities, racing deviated somewhat from this pattern. We see this from a letter by Ferdinand de Lesseps to the French General Daumas. In it, de Lesseps describes a race held on July 25, 1836, in Cairo. He himself had the luck to win, on his Barb horse. It was run on a straight course of only three miles. Not ten but sixteen horses were entered. Four groups of four horses started the race, so it was actually four races with four winners. These four winners then had to race each other.

The majority of racehorses were 'Nejdis,' i.e., desert Arabians from the Nejd in central Arabia. Their ages ranged from 3½ to 9. De Lesseps won the race with his 9-year-old Barb.

Today, this Arabian horse sport is enthusiastically followed in Baghdad, Basra, Beirut, Amman, Bahrain, El Riyadh, Tunis, Cairo, Alexandria, etc.

In Cairo, races are held every Saturday and Sunday from October through June, or in Alexandria during the hot summer months. There are six or seven races in the afternoon, over distances from five furlongs to two miles. Exclusively purebred Arabians race. The betting is enthusiastic here, as I could see in person. That Egypt has a population of twelve million Copts (non-Muslims) may play a certain role in this.

During a weekend in 1972, I counted 18 races at the Heliopolis track, of which five were 1000 meters (about five furlongs), four were 1200 meters (about six furlongs), four were 1400 meters (about seven furlongs), three were 1600 meters (about one mile), and two were 1800 meters (about 1.1 mile). In all, 185 horses were entered, and ridden for purses of between 260 and 700 Egyptian pounds.

Breeding successful race horses must be quite profitable for Egyptian breeders.

Not only the typical racehorse breeders' horses are honored here. The world-famous Arabians from El Zahraa, the Hamdan Stables, and the Tahawi also defend their colors on the racetracks at Heliopolis and Cairo. As I sat in the grandstand awaiting the next race, I automatically thought of the European Arabian breeders. How many of them speak disparagingly of racing Arabians, not recognizing that the pride of the classic asil Arabian's pedigree are names are of just such racing Arabs? I mention only IBN RADBAN, NAZEER, MASHAAN, IBN FAKHRI, SHAHRIAR, etc. They were all bred or raised by the Royal Agricultural Society (the Egyptian Agricultural Organization after 1952), at El Zahraa. If one bears in mind that NAZEER, as well as his son, IBN FAKHRI "KORAYEM," were successful racehorses like many other renowned state stud horses, one may ask whether breeding goals today should be more directed toward performance for mares, too – and not just toward beauty.

Noble Arabian birth and successful racing careers could very well go hand in hand. FOL GAMIL and MARSHALL (bred by Hamdan Stables) attest to this, among others. These two grey stallions, also famous for their beauty, won six and twelve races respectively on the track at Heliopolis.

From Cairo, we turn to the racetrack on the edge of the capital city of Jordan, Amman. It is a simple sand track. Flags signal the start. But what an atmosphere! What a difference between this and the tracks in Cairo and Beirut! There is no international crowd on display. No, here one is among the sons of the desert, Bedouins with their native desert horses.

Habes Pasha el Majali, sheikh of an influential Bedouin tribe and commander-in-chief of the Jordanian army, is president of the Royal Racing Club. H.R.H. Sharif Nasser ben Jamil,

BADIAH, the famous Abbayah mare of Prince Sharif Nasser ben Jamil. Badiah was winner of 2400 meter races, even when five months in foal.

AL SAAFIN, BADIAH's son.
In the winner's circle
for the twelfth time here,
at the racetrack in Beirut.
Photograph: Sharif Nasser ben Jamil.

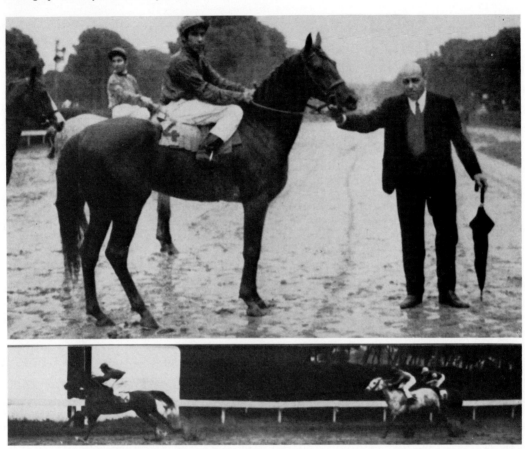

uncle of the king and previous commander-in-chief, is the patron. This afternoon there will be five races for purebred Arabians, and one for the famous racing camels. The military supervision is noticeable here. The few foreign guests are well-protected against any eventuality. Heavily-armed Bedouins are everywhere.

The races begin exactly at the time given in the program. First, three races for novices at 1000 meters – about five furlongs. Since a simple Bedouin with only one horse wouldn't have a chance in a field of horses from the famous stables, there are separate divisions for the simple man's horses and those from the big stables. How enormously large the stables can be is indicated by H.R.H. Sharif Nasser ben Jamil's stable of five hundred purebred Arabians. The Majali Bedouin sheikhs are also counted among the great breeders. Their horses run against those of the royal house. King Hüessein's mother, Sherifieh Zaim has Arabians, too, and sends them to the track. Stallions and mares race against each other. So in the second race, two mares and six stallions are running, and in the third, a novice race for the big stables, three stallions and three mares are entered. Even mares in foal may race, in exceptional circumstances.

Prince Sharif Nasser ben Jamil's favorite mare, a dark bay Abayyah, BADIA, won fame on the racetrack in Amman. An immensely rich businessman from Beirut came to Amman with his best Lebanese-Iraqi racehorses to show the Jordanians how it was done: Only Prince Sharif Nasser had a desert horse in a position to beat the Iraqi – the desert Abayyah mare, BADIAH. The only problem was that BADIAH was five months in foal. Completely convinced of the unbelievable toughness of his desert-raised asil Arabians, Sharif Nasser didn't hesitate to let his favorite run the race.

The small, wiry desert Arabians of Sheikh Habes el Majali and the beautiful, pregnant BADIAH, with their Bedouin jockeys, were at the start of the 2400 meter race. The Lebanese jockeys, sitting high on their tall Iraqi racehorses, looked disdainfully down at the small competitors. The flag dropped and they were off! The tension in the grandstand was almost unbearable. Just before the last turn, the Iraqis were still in the lead, with Habes el Majali's grey close behind. BADIAH's jockey masterfully swung her to the inside of the turn. They hit the homestretch. Without a whip used, they lengthened their strides. Necks stretched as they gave their all in the killing sprint to the finish. She was head to head with the leading Iraqi. The unbelievable happened – it was as if she was flying without wings. The Iraqi lagged behind. She quickened her pace still more. A hundred yards to go. Then ten.

She thundered past the finish three lengths in front of the Iraqi. The Bedouins went crazy. BADIAH had defended their honor – with a vengence!

Now, 13 years later, I'm standing next to BADIAH in her stall. She shoves her muzzle into my hand curiously. Well, OK, here's a sugar cube. She pricks her ears, sensing my great admiration. How beautiful she is! Her coat is as fine as the finest satin. Her legs are as clean as a 3-year-old's. Unbelievable. Standing outside later, she graciously allowed me to take her picture. "How did it go with your foal, then, Your Highness?" "I'll show you." Sharif Nasser takes me to the office above the stables. The walls are covered with racing photos. BADIAH foaled with no trouble – a stud colt, AL SAAFIN. He has become a triumphant racehorse. Sharif Nasser takes a picture from the wall. "Here, Dr. Klynstra, is her "foal' just before his twelfth win. I give you this picture as a memento of the splendid BADIAH."

Sharif Nasser breeds his future racehorses in his own way. The foals stay on the dam for about five months. The mares are ridden daily in the open for about an hour. The foals accompany them, developing their muscles and, equally important, getting to know the big, wide world. If the mare is over 15 years old, the foal is taken off her at three months and nourished with camels' milk. These young, newly-weaned horses are kept in rather small pens, preventing over-exertion. Too much exercise would be harmful to their young joints.

Half a year later, when the foals are ten to twelve months old, they are brought to a large, walled pasture. They live here with the swift gazelles. The gazelles, about the size of a deer, flit through the corral. The yearlings playfully race after them, matching speed. At dawn and sunset especially, this becomes an earnest race. Such play steels their muscles, develops speed, heart, and wind. Small portals in the wall offer the gazelles a chance to escape their pursuers. Such an escape door is particularly welcome when a herd of yearlings take up the chase and surround the gazelles. During this period, the yearlings are untouched by man. Unhaltered, ungroomed, they can run and play and laze and roll in the sand to their hearts' content. But contact – pleasant contact with man is not completely lost. Grooms hand feed them dates every day, speaking kindly to them.

At twenty months, they are made familiar with the saddle. The young animals are led around, and saddled, always calmly and lovingly and patiently. After feeding the yearlings bread soaked in date juice, they are bitted for the first time and left in the stall for a few hours to get use to it. If all goes well, the future racehorses are quietly backed.

During the next forty-five days, they will be ridden at a walk for longer and longer distances. This walking training develops the muscles excellently, without straining the tendons. Sharif Nasser demonstrated this with his own horses which had just recently completed their walking training. Their forearm muscles were particularly well-developed, hard as steel. After the walking conditioning comes the galloping conditioning. This training lasts nine months in all. At three years of age, then, the young horse is brought to the racetrack. It will run the 1000 meters for novices. Once it has won in the novice division, it enters the "third division." This division is further subdivided into divisions for horses up to or over four years old. Winners in the third division move to the second division. Should they win in this division, they must immediately prove themselves in the first division. These divisions take the place of a handicap system.

This system of divisions is also known at the *Societe piur la protection et Vamelioration de la race chevaline Arabe du Liban's* Hippodrome de Beyrouth, the racetrack at Beirut. Nevertheless, there is a great difference between Beirut and Amman. The Lebanese track is much larger, and has a more international character. The typical Arabic atmosphere does not reign there. Bedouins are hardly ever seen. One could easily mistake oneself to be in France. The start can be observed from the boxes via monitors.

Behind the grandstand are the stables. A seven century-old triumphal arch of truly eternal green ficus offers a topic of conversation with the Marquis Moussa de Freige. This remarkable arch was planted in the 13th century by Prince Fakhreddine for the track's champion horse. The track at Beirut is already seven hundred years old.

The Marquis de Freige personally showed us his racehorses. He is the proud owner of about 200 "purebred Arabians." The white stables lie among dark green Lebonese pines. Blooming bougainvilleas in the pleasant shade delight the eye. Grooms lead an unbroken stream of horses past us. All of them are purebred Arabians, the Marquis explains to us. We stare at the horses, a bit bewildered. They are generally much larger and heavier than the Jordanian desert Arabians, and are less classic, less typey. But some among them are splendidly Arabian. As a large, roman-nosed racehorse is led past us, one of the observers comments that it resembled a true Hanoveraner more than an Arabian. Overhearing the comment, the Marquis de Freige notes kindly, if with rather a harsh undertone, that "the mistake you Europeans make is that you have only one type of Arabian in your head, although there are really about 200 different types."

The royal mares' stables in Amman,
Jordan.

111

The large, coarse Iraqis are officially allowed on the racetrack with Arabians. They often have English Thoroughbred and Persian blood as well as Arabian. That explains much, if not all. Later, when visiting the stud farm of Marquis de Freige, Prince Mansour ben Saoud and Bey Pharoan we saw many typey, lovely Arabian mares with foals, but also saw some mares with roman noses.

On Sunday afternoon, we were invited to the races by the chairman, Bey Henri Pharoan. Eight races were held: two at 1000 meters, two at 1400 meters, and four at 1600 meters. Ninety-eight horses were entered, and purses totaled about 36,000 Lebanese pounds. When we arrived, the track teamed with testy, grim-looking, heavily armed soldiers. There is much unrest in Lebanon. During the night, Palentinians had bombed the Jordanian embassy in Beirut, and the airport had had bomb threats.

Despite the unrest, the racetrack was full. The VIP box had been reserved for us. The second race was about to start: a Prix de Zaghdaraya for the novice division, three-year-olds to carry 114 pounds, and four-year-olds, 125 pounds – a combination division and handicap system. The three-year-old RODA won the 1000 meters in 1:09.8. That was not especially fast. On January 13, FAHKRI ran the 1000 meters in 1:07. The next race began in half an hour. We walked around a bit. This was not much different than an European racetrack. An elegant, international crowd. Long rows at the betting windows. Up to 500 Lebanese pounds can be bet here. Whereas the races at Amman were popular entertainment, the Beirut races were more an ice-cold business. The purses were appopriate to the atmosphere. H.R.H. Prince Mansour ben Saoud from Saudi Arabia, for example, bought the stallion, AMIR EL ZEMANI, for about $ 28,000. Two days later, the stallion earned back his purchase price on this track.

To give an idea of the Arabian racehorse's speed, I have sought out a few track records for 2000 meters (1¼ miles), for comparison with the time of the English Thoroughbred, Run Home S.:

Run Home S., Engl. T.B., Netherlands	2:14.1
Nasr, Arabian, Egypt, 1924	2:20
Sartez, Arabian, U.S.A., 1948	2:17.1
Primevere, Arabian, Tunysia	2:12
Karagos, Arabian, Poland	2:14.5

The fastest Thoroughbreds are much faster than the fastest Arabian. This is clearly shown by comparison of the time for the 100th German Derby with those of some Arabians track records for 2400 meters (one and a half miles):

Don Giovanni, Eng. T. B., Germany, 1971	2:33.1
Sart, Arabian, Poland, 1937	2:49
Sartez, Arabian, U.S.A., 1948	2:46.5
El Haddag, Arabian, Egypt, 1972	2:44.6

Had these four raced each other, Don Giovanni would have won with a lead of almost one furlong. The record times posted by Arabians in Poland differ only slightly from those run in the rest of the world. The Polish record holder's bloodlines are very different from domestic Polish Arabians, as described in Guttman and Klynstra's book, *The Lineage of Polish Arabians* (1968). The Polish record-holder for 2800 meters (1¾ mile), for example, is by the French imported stallion, KHARTOUM, a son of the desert Arabian, EL SBAA. The stallion KARAGOS record-holder for 2000 meters (1¼ mile), was a son of the desert Arabian, ALI PASZA; IKWA and MINARET, record-holders at 1800 (1.1 miles) and 2600 meters (1.6 miles) respectively, are both sons of the Hungarian asil Arabian stallion, KOHEILAN I, while the famous SART, Polish record-holder for 2400 meters (1½ miles) is by the asil NEDJARI, bred in France.

Looking at the average times for Polish-bred horses, as given by Flade, we see that the Polish and Russian Arabians are slower than others at 1600 meters (1 mile):

Egyptian Arabians	1:49.6
British-Indian Arabians	1:50.0
Russian Arabians	1:55.0
Polish Arabians	1:55.2

Over a 1600 meter track, then, the Polish and Russian Arabians would have been about 70 meters (over 20 lengths – tr.) behind the Egyptian and British-Indian Arabians. One might well wonder whether this loss of speed is traceable to their mixture of foreign blood. This is assumed to be the case among the English Thoroughbred circles. The difference between the individual racetracks is not a significant factor, since the track records are all on the same level.

Comparisons of track records points out yet another interesting fact. One frequently reads that Mu'niqi are the true racehorses among Arabians. In one of his many letters to me, my friend, Robert Mauvy, president of the Syndicat des Eleveurs et Amateur du cheval Arabe, contested this idea with the words: "If the Mu'niqi were indeed the fastest horses, the Bedouins would never have trained or used anything else."

True, the Mu'niqi resemble the English Thoroughbred in appearance more than they do the classic Arabian types such as the Kuhaylan and Saqlawi, and the Thoroughbred is indeed the fastest horse in the world. However, if we look at the Egyptian record-holder for 1200 and 2000 meters, NASR, we see that this fastest Arabian was not only not Mu'niqi, but that he didn't have a drop of Mu'niqi blood. NASR was an asil Kuhaylan-Jallabi.

The successful EUPHRATES (Bombay, 1881) was a Koheilan om Soura, according to Wilfrid Scawen Blunt. The famous racing Arabian, GREYLEG, who won 51 races in Bombay, was a desert-bred Koheilan, according to Tweedie.

How is it that these Kuhaylans have had such great success on the track, while the Mu'niqi are supposed to be faster? Was Mauvy right when he said that it was a common fiction that the Mu'niqi are the fastest?

I would like to conclude this section on Arabian racehorses by reporting the fastest time I could find in the literature about the subject. In 1948, SARTEZ, bred by Carl Raswan, ran the quarter mile in 0:23.25, a speed of 38.6 miles per hour.

115

Nuri Sha'lān,
Prince of the Ruala
Photograph:
C. R. Raswan

CHAPTER IX

EL ASIL/THE PUREBRED

The Arabian horse is a breed adapted to the Bedouins' hard life in the desert through inbreeding and strict natural selection. Compared to other breeds, it needs much less food, can go longer without water, has greater endurance, and is far better able to withstand great variations in temperature. However it may be more susceptible to high humidity.

Let us ask ourselves: what would happen if these asil desert horses were to be crossed with Western horses?

To better understand, we should first investigate a few other natural breeds which, like the Arabian, have adapted themselves to life under highly unfavorable climatic conditions. Results of crossing these breeds with foreign blood should demonstrate an important point for our desert horses, too.

North of Scotland, the Shetland Islands form an archipelago of 117 islands. The ground is rocky, and partly covered with a thick marsh. The marshes support some mosses and heather, but neither grows over a few inches tall. The rocky coasts produce seaweeds. The climate is very unpleasant – an extreme maritime type, with cool summers and mild winters, but windy and stormy. Not a day passes without some form of precipitation – drenching rains in the summer, and snowstorms in the winter. Sunshine is very rare indeed. Such a climate is extremely poor for horses. Yet, the Shetland ponies have thrived there for centuries. No one knows where they came from, but it is certain that large herds of them dwelled there by the 6th century A.D. Over the centuries, they have led a very hard life. When conditions were at their worst, the local people would feed a single herd of their draft ponies. The other ponies sought shelter along the coasts during the winter and tried to keep themselves alive on seaweed. But not too many could reach the coast, for Nature would claim her victims when surprise snowstorms caught them in the interior. Foodless, they would try to reach the coastal refuge, climbing the snow-covered rocks and crevasses. Not every animal managed it.

In the 19th century, the Shetland ponies were discovered to be good draft animals for the English coal mines. Demand for the ponies grew quickly. As usual in such a case, several people thought of "improving" the breed, in the hopes of earning more money from them.

On Mainland Island, Fjord breeding stallions were introduced, creating the larger Sumburgh strain. Its descendants survived for a certain time, but eventually died out completely. In 1855, Arthur Nicholson started cross-breeding with a Mustang and an Arabian stallion. He was therefore relying on two breeds accustomed to dry climates, not this humidity and cold. The result of the experiment was the Feltar strain, standing about 118 cm.

The Sumburgh and Feltar strains deviated greatly from the original Shetland type. They lacked the hardiness and iron constitution which would have enabled them to survive in their exceedingly cold, wet world. The cross-breeds could not stand up to the hard life on the Shetland Islands, and died out (*Colenbrander*, 1969).

A further example can be found in the Carpathian Mountains forests bordering the Ukraine, Poland, Hungary, and Rumania, a highly inaccessible, rugged region with peaks soaring to 2663 m. This is the home range of a mountain-type horse breed, the Huzules. The Huzule is an independent, well-consolidated breed with its own typical build, behavior, and character. As a natural race, it is closely related to the wild horses. For centuries, the Carpathian's inaccessibilty has favored inbreeding and purebreeding among these mountain horses, which have become established as a consolidated, prepotent breed. Over hundreds of years, the inexorable environmental conditions have acted as a selective culling force. The Huzule of the high mountains never sees oats, of course; in the winter, it scrapes away the snow to get at the grass. The original Huzule is an extremely good doer. During the previous century, the Austro-Hungarian monarchy recognized the military value of these mountain horses, and began to influence them under a state-controlled breeding program. Their success was not always consistent, nor obvious. Here, too, the attempt was made to breed somewhat larger animals. Cross breeding with larger horses, however, caused the Huzule to lose its valued traits. The crossbreds were not up to the hard mountain life. On open pasture, without grain or stables, the breeding herds "purified" themselves of the foreign blood. The crossbreds starved, froze to death, or remained barren, and their foals born in the wild either died or fell to the wolves. In the end, only the original purebred Huzule survived (*Haberland*, 1969).

These results are in full agreement with what one might theoretically expect. Crossbreds are usually less well-adapted to their parents' native environment. Therefore, even when the hybrid offspring are very fertile, selection will be weighted against them, thus limiting their propagation. But if, for whatever reason, the environment should change drastically, the

A fascinating beauty with a distinct maternal expression: SAEMAH (Madkour I – El Samraa), Winner Asil Cup Mares, Dillenburg and also Arab Horse Show

Gieboldehausen 1985 and 1986. Bred and owned by Peter Gross, D-3173 Müden-Dieckhorst
Photograph: S. Kübe

advantage could swing in favor of the crossbreds, which would then reproduce easily (*Mettler & Gregg*, 1969).

Our Arabian horses have been confronted with just such a radical change in environment. The desert horses were brought to our humid, warm climate from a world subject to lack of water, famine, and extreme thermal fluctuations, where temperatures may drop 80°F within 15 minutes. When brought to our regions, animals accustomed to living outdoors summer and winter became pampered stable-dwellers allowed to eat their fill in lovely, rich pastures only under favorable weather conditions. Foals in particular benefited from this change: foal mortality which stood at roughly 50% among the Bedouins' herds was reduced to about 10% in our regions. Weak animals, too, survived and reproduced themselves. While environmental selection under the murderous desert conditions is extremely harsh, and crossbreds such as Anglo-Arabians are eliminated with lightning speed, this automatic self-cleansing process does not take place in our civilized world. One could even anticipate that selection would be directed against the Arabian when crossing Arabians and European or American horses in our environment.

In addition, many European breeders prefer certain physical characteristics in their European saddle-horses, and distain the desert-bred Arabian's traits. Some breeders like their Arabians somewhat or even very much larger. Others prefer a long back or rounded croup. Quite incorrectly, many even consider the light bone to be a sign of weakness, and such opinions again influence breeding to the disadvantage of the desert type. Cold and humidity play their role, too, as natural selective factors in Europe. Diseases such as heaves occur here, although they are practically unknown in Arabia, which channels selection in another direction here again.

Polish Arabian horse breeding before 1930 is the perfect example of such a situation. In *The Lineage of the Polish Arabian Horse,* Guttman and Klynstra, analyse Polish purebreds' bloodlines back to the 12th generation. During the first decades of the 19th century, this strain was produced from native Polish horses and a considerable percentage of Arabian blood. Aside from these two breeds, the pedigrees from this period also include English Thoroughbred, Turkoman, and Persian horses, as well as many of unknown origin. Although many Arabian desert-breds were used for breeding, the fact remains that many part-bred Arabians and part-bred Anglo-Arabs were crossed with each other in this 'pure' breeding. Thorough study of the pedigrees published in the above mentioned book should convince any skeptic.

The famous "purebred" Arabian stallion, DARDZILING (1903) is a fine example of how "purebred" Arabians were being produced at that time in Poland. This stallion had some 90 % ascertainable Arabian blood. Other "purebred" Arabians from that period with lesser percentage of ascertainable Arabian blood are known, such as ARABELLA (1898), grand-dam of ADAMAS (1930) and of ARABESKA (1931). Only 37½ % of this mare's blood was actually traceable as being Arabian (see *Guttmann & Klynstra*, 1968, pedigree # 3). On the other hand, some Polish Arabians were truly asil, i.e., of 100 % traceable Arabian blood, but they were the exceptions and unfortunately can no longer be found today. A closer look at DARDZILING, again, gives us the following information. His four grandparents were:

Achmed Ejub (1881)
Delia (1884)
Antar (D.B.)
Dulcinea (1894)

Of these four ancestors, only ANTAR is an original, desert-bred Arabian. The other three must be considered part-bred Anglo-Arabs.

Looking at ACHMED EJUB's 16 great-grandparents behind these three grandparents, we see that

ACHMED EJUB's ancestry includes:
2 part-bred Anglo-Arabs; and,
1 half-bred Arab;
DELIA's ancestry includes:
4 part-bred Anglo-Arabs; and,
4 half-bred Arabians;
DULCINEA's ancestry includes:
3 part-bred Anglo-Arabs; and,
3 half-bred Arabians.

Crossing these various part-breds with each other occasioned widely varying breeding results. The get included horses of extreme Arabian type as well as many throwbacks to the non-Arabian ancestors. These crossbreds, however, were not eliminated in the Polish environment; the desert horse population was not automatically purified of foreign blood. Also lacking was any consistent re-breeding to desert Arabians to displace the throwbacks. Quite the contrary – part-breds were even bred to part-breds.

Carl R. Raswan (2nd from right) with the
Ruala. At his side Prince Fuaz.
Photograph: Archiv E. Raswan

Measurements of 88 Polish Arabians foaled between 1899 and 1929 definitely show the part-bred characteristics of these "purebred" Arabians. The height, girth, and bone were used to calculate a caliber index illustrating the ratio of trunk and bone to height. The following table gives the statistics for purebred Arabians from various countries, as well as for other breeds and races:

Caliber Index for Asil and Purebred Arabians (Ar) and Other Breeds and Races

Asil Arabians (Arabia Deserta and Egypt)	130
France (Ar)	137
Romania (Ar)	138
Germany (Ar)	140
English Thoroughbred	140
Hungary (Ar)	141
Bulgaria (Ar)	142
Spain (Ar)	144
Great Britain (Ar)	144
Soviet Union (Ar)	146
Poland, 1936–1956 (Ar)	148
Half-Bred Arabian	150
Poland, 1899-1929 (Ar)	152
Trakehner	154
Lippizzaner	159
Polish Konik	160

This table clearly shows that, according to the caliber index, Polish purebred Arabians foaled between 1899 and 1929 resemble the part-bred Arabian, and also that those foaled between 1936 and 1956 are not essentially different. The foreign blood's influence is even outwardly visible, and far from eliminated.

Around 1930, 3 desert-bred stallions: KOHEILAN HAIFI D.B., KOHEILAN AFAS D.B., and KOHEILAN KRUSZAN D.B.; as well as French asil Arabian stallions such as NEMER and KHARTOUM (both sons of EL SBAA, D.B.) were stood at stud. Polish breeders' expert selection of breeding stock partially succeeded in recapturing the Arabian

The ostrich banner and the Prophet's Flag.
Photograph: C. R. Raswan

type. As the Table above shows, the caliber index was reduced from 152 to 148 within 20 years, i.e., between 1936 an 1956. Compared to the asil desert and Egyptian Arabians' scores, it is still too high, but this could be due in part to their soil type. (Seydel, 1933, p. 75; Bilke, 1976, p. 81). The use of asil Arabian stallions led to other positive results which do not appear in the caliber index. For instance, the average trunk length was shortened from 57.3 inches (1899-1929) to 56.5 inches (1936-1956), and the girth increased over the same period from 66.3 inches to 68.6 inches (see Chapter IV). These data regarding Polish Arabians conclusively prove the great value of pure blood for Arabian breeders. The environmental culling which protected the Shetland pony on its islands, the Huzule in the Carpathians, and the Arabian in the desert against the long term influence of foreign blood is totally lacking in western Europe's moderate climate. Centralized governmental breeding programs such as are carried out in Poland can restrict the damage done by cross-breeding to foreign blood, by expert use of asil blood. However, this task is not simple in most other countries with their many small, private breeders. What breeder, for instance will withdraw his broodmare from breeding because of some defect in type? Practically every executive committee of Arabian breed associations was therefore fully convinced that purebred Arabians must be of the purest bloodlines if breeding was to be successful. Hence, when developing their articles and by-laws, the definition of a purebred Arabian horse always required an uninterrupted line to desert-bred ancestors.

The Arab Horse Society of the United Kingdom founded in 1919, states in the *Memorandum and Articles of Association (1983)* that *"The term 'Arab or Arabian horse' shall mean those horses in whose pedigrees there is none than pure Arab blood."*

The former chairman of the Arab Horse Society, the well-known author Mr. *R. S. Summerhays, again stressed this definition of a purebred Arabian quite clearly in his book, The Arab Horse in Great Britain* (1967, p. 55): "...alien blood is unknown; indeed, should it be introduced, the result is that it at once becomes either Anglo-Arab or part-bred Arab." Based on this definition and Mr. Summerhays' statements, one would expect that no Arabian with any traceable foreign blood would be registered as purebred in the English studbook. The reality of the situation is quite different. When entering horses in the purebred registry, purity of blood was apparently not taken too accurately in England. Right at the start, in 1919, the beautiful and later so famous grey Polish stallion, SKOWRONEK, was

Albrecht Adam: King Wilhelm von Württemberg. Archiv H. H. Joachim Prinz zu Fürstenberg

registered as purebred in the English studbook, despite the fact that his dam, JASKOLKA, had foreign blood in her pedigree, namely:

  5 times English Thoroughbred
  2 times Turkoman
16 times native Polish mares: Kobyla (5 x)
                               Demianka (2 x)
                               Kwiata (3 x)
                               Woloszka
                               Milordska
                               Sawicka
                               Szejkowska
                               Anielka
                               Ilniecka

Documented foreign ancestors of JASKOLKA dam of SKOWRONEK. – see *Guttmann & Klynstra*, 1968, Pedigree II.

After this initial Polish importation, several other imported Arabians with traceable foreign blood arrived. They, too, were registered without further ado as purebred Arabians.

The English studbook offers a few more interesting facts. Horses with successful track careers in India were imported from the Far East. Of these horses, often:

  a) the origin was unknown;
  b) the strain was unknown,;
  c) the breeder was unknown;
  d) the country of origin was unknown; and
  e) occasionally, even the year of birth was unknown.

Although nothing was known about these horses aside from the remark "for racing" or "winner of races," etc., they were registered in the English studbook as purebreds.

    A few such examples are:
    CHANDI (Vol. I, p. 35, "for racing"),
    CROSBIE (Vol. I, p. 36, "winner of races"),
    and ZOOWAR (Vol. I, p. 79, "winner of races").

Nothing whatsoever indicates that these racehorses acquired in India had Arabian blood, much less that they were purebred! Such cases are not limited to the beginnings of the English Arab Horse Society; they can still be found today. Let's take a look at the *Arab Horse Studbook*, Vol. VIII (1957), p. 39. The following horse is registered as purebred:

SAHIL, Ch. (1942), Neget.

Desert-bred. Pedigree unknown.

Breeder unknown. Owner Mr. D.E.M.

Strain unknown. Pedigree unknown. Breeder unknown. Only his color, year of foaling, and English owner are known. This is therefore a horse without one single percentage of traceable Arabian blood, but which nevertheless was registered as purebred Arabian.

Hence, the Arab Horse Society Show catalogue for 1976 falsely states on p. 10 that "Arabian horses are those in whose pedigrees there is none other than pure Arabian blood."

In Germany, too, foreign blood frequently found its way into the Arabian breed. The stallion mentioned previously, DARDZILING, for instance, stood at stud in Weil in 1913. As we have seen, only 89 % of his blood was ascertainably Arabian. After World War II, quite a few Polish Arabians with foreign blood were used at stud in Germany. Therefore, in 1967, only a very few German Arabians conformed with the strict statutory rules of the Gesellschaft der Züchter und Freunde des Arabischen Pferdes e.V. (Society of Breeders and Friends of the Arabian Horse): *"In accordance with breeding goals, purebred Arabian horses are those which demonstrably trace back exclusively to desert-bred Arabians. Those horses will be registered which have incontestable proof of such parentage."*

As a logical consequence, NIGRA-ZSCHEIPLITZ, foundation mare of the Arabian stud farm, Roblingen, was excluded from the AV studbook, together with all her offspring. *"Upon subsequent investigation, the responsible gentlemen of the German Arabian Association discovered a small flaw in NIGRA-ZSCHEIPLITZ's pedigree, namely seven generations back through her sire, MAZUD. With great courage and laudable correctness, they eliminated the mare and all of her descendents from the purebred Arabian registery, and declared them to be of Arabian, though not purebred, blood. However admirable such a procedure may seem, it is regrettable that the gentlemen did not extend their worthwile investigations to other Arabians. NIGRA-ZSCHEIPLITZ would not have been alone in her expulsion from paradise, but would have galloped across the threshold among a stately herd."* (Schiele, *Arabians in Europe*, 1967).

For 19 years, the Society issued pedigrees for purebred Arabians. After the Guttmann-Klynstra book (1968) proved that the registrations for Polish Arabians were not valid, the

Society altered the definition of purebred Arabian in September 1968 in such a way that everything could subsequently be legitimized.

It later read: *"In accordance with breeding goals, purebred Arabian horses are those which are recognized as such in their country of origin (country of birth), and are, or were, registered in its studbook for purebred Arabians..."*

Many more examples could be cited. So it is easy to understand why many horse breeders and experts feared that asil blood was dying out. Mauvy (1964) wrote in the conclusion of his book: *"It is absolutely essential and of the greatest importance to save what remains of the purebred Arabian. We must not let one of Creation's most beautiful works become endangered or even disappear ... I hope that friends and admirers of the purebred Arabian will unite and immediately take in hand the admirable but difficult task of saving the Arabian horse at any price. I beg them to do so, for tomorrow...tomorrow it will be too late..."*

Pure blood cannot be preserved if there is no clear distinction between asil Arabians and Arabians with foreign blood. The first step in the right direction was taken by an American, Mrs. Jane L. Ott. She published *The Blue Arabian Horse Catalog* in 2 volumes. Volume I had already appeared in 1961, a work whose significance for the Arabian world cannot be overestimated. This catalogue contains all American asil Arabians, as well as the asil imports to the USA. Considering that, through ignorance, asil mares were covered by non-asil stallions, by 1956, the number of asil foals in the entire American Arabian breeding stock was down to ten. Raswan and J. L. Ott deserve thanks for preserving asil breeding in the USA.

On the basis of the discoveries made by Mrs. Jane L. Ott, Carl R. Raswan, Ursula Guttmann and Foppe B. Klynstra, two associations persistently took charge of conserving the Bedouin tradition, the breeding of Arabian horses with asil stock:

The *Asil Club* with its head office in Germany, and presently members from 24 countries; and the *Al Khamsa, Inc.* in the USA. Both have clearly declared that the goal of every Arabian breeding program should be:

To breed with pure blood, to breed asil.

Furthermore, the *Asil Club* also supports selection by performance tests. Obviously, the pure Arabian of desert type, with its free, smart action is to be preferred, and the reknown good character of the asil Arabian must be demonstrated.

Founding the Asil Club is credited to Dr. h.c. W. Georg Olms, who, on September 10, 1974, assembled a number of pureblood breeders in Freiberg, West Germany, and promoted the

Asil Cup International 1986 at the Hessian
State Stud Dillenburg
Winner of the Asil Cup: MESSAOUD
(Madkour – Maymoonah)

Breeder: Seydlitz
Owner: Chrymont.

pure lineage of Arabians among those with common interest in the matter. The term "purebred" was replaced by the internationally better-known expression "asil," defined by Raswan in his Index under No. 846 on page 53, Part I as:

Asil (fem. asal, pl. asayil) – pure, original, genuine. An authentic Arabian horse kept PURE from the "root."

Experts of the Arabic language will know that asil (pronounced a-zil, accent on the 2nd syllable) means pure, authentic, thoroughbred, unadulterated. Any Arab, especially any horse breeder, associates this word with the pure origin of an animal or even a person.

The Asil Club is an association of breeders and friends of the asil Arabian which adopts the Bedouins' old, reliable breeding rules. The Club defines its objective as follows: "The Asil Arabian is a horse whose pedigree is exclusively based on Bedouin breeding, without any crossbreeding with non-Arabian horses at any time. The word 'asil' is derived from the Arabic language and means pure, true, noble and genuine."

The publication of its document, *Asil Arabians: The Noble Arabian Horses, III,* is a special contribution by the Asil Club. This book has been praised as the "most beautiful studbook of all times." With this work available in English, German, and Arabic, the Asil Club has erected a monument. It is important because here, unlike anywhere else, persuasive testimony has been collected which documents, in the first place, the great importance of asil breeding, and it accents all elements which distinguish the Arabian horse. The importance of tradition; the influence of Arabic culture and science on the Western world; and, the essence of the Bedouin, the 'Knights of the Desert', are especially brought home by the author and publisher, *Dr. h.c. W. Georg Olms.* He was honoured by an invitation to Saudi Arabia by the crown prince, where he was awarded a medal at the hand of *H. R. H. Prince Badr Ben Abdulaziz,* Vice Chairman of the Equestrian Club and of the National Guard. In a letter from the President of the King Faisal Foundation, *H.R.H. Prince Chaled Al Feisal* said the following:

"This work accentuates that the asil Arabian horse is a product of the Arabian peninsula and not, as some people maintain, the result of breeding improvements made by others, non-Arabic countries. It explains Bedouin traditions in breeding asil horses and their importance when establishing other breeds of horses. One chapter is dedicated to the influence of Arabic-islamic sciences and civilization on the Western world, another one to the essence of the noble

*Under the flags of Saudi Arabia and
Germany the show-class with the fillies is
starting in the early morning,
ASIL CUP INTERNATIONAL 1988,
Ludwigsburg Castle*

*A great event: For the first time in Europe
an Arabian Horse Show took place in front
of such a wonderful background and in the
midst of the "Flowering Baroque"
exhibition, under the patronage of
Ministerpräsident Dr. Lothar Späth.*

horsemen of the desert and their love of asil horses. It is a pleasure to study this work with its subjects and valuable as well as interesting information.

(Note: H.R.H. Prince Chaled is the governor of the province of Asir in the Kingdom of Saudi-Arabia and the President of the King Feisal Foundation, he is expert of merits and the owner of the most esteemed breed of valuable falcons in the Arabian countries.)

In his Foreword, no less a personage than State Equerry *Dr. G. Wenzler* commented that:

Extraordinary breeding measures had to be taken in order to save the pure, classical Arabian horse from decline. To this end it was necessary to form a breeding elite such as Raswan had spoken of, but this was considered an illusion ignorant of the world, a barren theory. Only eventually some courageous breeders became acquainted with the idea of falling back upon the old breeding methods of the Bedouin and gathering the few model asil Arabians still in existence. They meant to form a reservoir of pure blood for the regeneration of the Arabian horse. In the Federal Republic of Germany a small number of far-sighted and determined breeders in 1974 founded the Asil Club which was to take care of the pure breeding of the Arabian horse. As early as in 1977 this breeders' association, which in the meantime had become international, was able to publish the Asil Arabian Documentation.
By means of ample illustrations contributed by the members and statements taken from publications of old and new experts in horses, the character and the performance of the classical Arabian horse were presented. Now an ever increasing number of open-minded breeders also became convinced that the pure-bred Arabian horse equalled his ancestor, the desert Arabian, in the best possible way as to performance and character. All merits – endurance, intelligence, modesty of demands – are combined in him.
The list of honorary members is impressive. They are led by the Honorary President of the Asil Club, *Douglas B. Marshall,* presently an honorary director and previously president of the Arabian Horse Registry of America, as well as a member of its governing board for over twenty years and former president of the Pyramid Society, among other honours. A great number of renowned breeders from twenty-four countries are outspoken advocates of the old, traditional Bedouin breeding methods.

The great mares of El Zahraa:
OM EL SAAD (Shaloul – Yashmak)

MONIET EL NEFOUS
(Shaloul – Wanisa)

The Asil Club has set a new standard with the *Asil Cup International*. True to its goals, these remarkable horse shows were held in 1985 and 1986 at the Hessian State Stallion Center at Dillenburg, West Germany, and included the Arabian's most suitable performance test for Arabian horses: the long-distance ride. The art exhibits were also much admired. Paintings, engravings, graphics, and bronzes of the Arabian horse by 19th century masters were exhibited in 1985, and works by contemporary artists were shown in 1986.

In 1986, the first Saudi Arabian astronaut, *H.R.H. Prince Sultan Bin Salman Bin Abdulaziz*, was the patron of the show. The Asil Club's standing was established among such personages as the ambassador of the Kingdom of Saudi Arabia *H.E. Abbas Al-Ghazzawy*, *H.R.H. Prince Chaled Al Suderi*, and the ambassador of the Hashemite kingdom of Jordan, *H.E. Sharif Fawaz Sharaf*. The Saudi Arabian television carried the event to the Arabian peninsula on six different satellite broadcasts.

Yet another word on the three-type-theory: again and again one meets here blind trust or – although seldom – prejudice. This often parallels the veneration or even idolization of *Carl R. Raswan* on the one hand, or the denunciation of this enthusiast and expert on the other hand – who is then frequently called Carl Schmidt, as if his German descent were a fault.

"Aside from General von Pettko-Szandter, I don't know any other Arabian expert in our century who has done more for and so fostered the asil Arabian horse than the German, Carl R. Raswan. He spent may years with the Bedouins, and had the opportunity to study the manners, the customs, and especially the Arabian horses with the individual tribes. The works by Klaus, Käselau, and Oppenheim, who, like Raswan, lived with the Bedouins, and the works by Brown, Davenport, Seidel, and others, confirm that Raswan had observed excellently and gives in his books exact renderings of the Bedouins' lives. No one but him had observed so many horses in the Arabic countries and captured them in written record." (Olms)

Not even an Arab is known who had examined, compared, and studied, like Raswan did, the stock worldwide and especially in the Arabian peninsula, who had also studied the old Arabic manuscripts dealing with Arabian horses. While he agreed with the three-type-

His pedigree shows the great Nazeer sons Kaisoon, Hadban Enzahi and Ghazal: Top Ten stallion MANAR (Maymoon – Maamounah), bred by Seidlitz, owned by W. Isbert, D-5411 Eitelborn, on lease at Olms Stud.

theory, it may be unknown to many – even to Arabs themselves – and it is evident to a scholar of equine matters. Saqlawi, Kuhaylan, and Mu'niqi – these are the three extreme types.

"As in every breed of horse, the Arabian horses are divided into two largely differing types: those whose duty it is to preserve the refinement and temperament of the race and those who are to preserve the more practical qualities. Wherever there are a great many stallions of different breeds together in official studs, it is simple to distinguish these two basic types. In the Arabian breed, too, the first category is known and necessary for beauty and refinement, race and delicate modeling, wiriness and expressiveness whereas the second category shows a more practical horse who transmits and preserves sturdiness, broad chest, ample girth, strong bones and a high conversion of food. An example of the first type is the very refined Saqlavi, the second is the firm and practical Kuhaylan." (Bilke)

Raswan, however, added another to these two basic types: the Mu'niqi, an Arabian which, with its long lines, could well be thought as having good qualities for short races; a horse not always very convincing in type, which, according to Raswan's judgements, seldom showed the desired results when mated with the other basic types – the Kuhaylan and Saqlawi.

What we are familiar with are mostly mixed types. This applies also to pedigrees. But maintaining the three types in their distinct forms should be the goal of each responsible Arabian horse breeder, rather than seeking an unvarying Arabian that he might like to present as the ideal type.

Do we really want to reject such horses as MORAFIC, KAISOON, or FARAG as markedly Saqlawi-type horses? Do we really want to reject such outstanding horses of the Kuhaylan-type as HADBAN ENZAHI, or horses like those bred at the Babson farm to succeed the splendid FADL? Happily, the Babson lines are just now coming more and more into international recognition and high honour.

One further worthy organization is the *Al Khamsa, Inc.,* , which, similar to the Asil Club, unequivocally intercedes for asil descent. It performed an excellent service with its publication, *Al Khamsa Arabians: A Documentation of Al Khamsa Arabians and Their History* (Rockford, IL; 1983), especially through its ardent members and presidents, *Jeanne and*

Charles Craver (renowned breeders of Davenport Arabians), *Joe Farris, Carol Neubauer, Richard Pritzlaff, Carol Schultz, Edna Weeks, Diana Weiner,* and others.

From that text we read: *"Al Khamsa is an organization of people devoted to furthering the survival of the asil horse of Bedouin-Arabia by means of education and research … The horses of primary interest to Al Khamsa are Bedouin-Arabians, defined as those that can be reasonably assumed to be descended entirely from horses bred in the Arabian desert by Bedouin tribes."*

We owe recognition to the *Pyramid Society* of the USA for having bestowed due respect and esteem on the Egyptian asil Arabians, which had not been at all highly regarded in the Commonwealth and the USA. We must say that the main force behind the new glory of Egyptian asil breeding was General Tibor von Pettko-Szandtner. Now, however, the sale of a great number of essential breeding animals after his time has weakened asil breeding in Egypt. It would be advisable now, as a few decades ago, to bring asilbred performance stallions in from Arabia Deserta and other countries. It is equally advisable to subject horses, or at least the stallions, principally to difficult performance tests such as were previously decisive, but which today are only partially carried out on Egyptian racetracks. If this were done, breeding could not be reproached for having beauty as its only goal. Remember: to breed only for beauty, to pander to aesthetics or even mere head-hunters, does not only risk degeneration – it enforces it. Breeding with just one objective in mind has always been accompanied by the degeneration of the neglected factors. This applies to all breeding, not just horse breeding. This cannot be overemphasized to horse breeders. The Pyramid Society deserves great recognition for having served the cause of Arabia Deserta's Bedouin asil breeding, that region being practically the exclusive source of Egypt's stock. Why asil horses which stem directly from the scource of the Arabia Deserta must first pass through Egypt, however, remains a puzzling inconsistency.

The following are the important paragraphs from the *Reference Handbook of Straight Egyptian Horses* published by the *Pyramid Society:*

"The Pyramid Society is a fraternal organization of people interested in Arabian horses of Egyptian bloodlines. The purposes of the Pyramid Society are to preserve and perpetuate Egyptian bloodlines as a nucleus of outcross blood and to encourage use of that outcross blood as a source of the classic refinement so necessary to the breed and for which the Egyptians are prepotently line-bred.

A remarkable stallion of the Abu Dhabi
Royal Stables: HAMASA NASRAN
(Farag – Shar Zarqa)
Bred by Olms Arabians Hamasa Stud

Owned by Sheikh Zayed Ben Sultan Al
Nahyan, President of the U.A.E.
Hamasa Nasran is full brother to Hamasa
Zarif, see page 82

The purpose of the Society in establishing a definition of an Arabian horse of "straight" Egyptian bloodlines and publishing a list of acknowledged root stock is for the guidance of its members."
Opinions of the Egyptians' asil Arabian breeding will, of course, vary. Its ups and downs, its blossoming and withering make it impossible to praise it exclusively, but considering these circumstances, the quality of such breeding stock is still to be rated higher.

What an incredible prepotency these asil Arabian horses have!

The noblest of horses could at times be seen here, but who counts the sacrifices inherent to such consolidation? What is left of these thousands of classic asil Bedouin horses? Almost nothing: not more than sixteen mares formed the first foundation stock for the Egyptian Agricultural Organization (E.A.O.), today the Royal Agricultural Society (R.A.S).

Recall that *Mohammed Ali* (1769–1849) collected Arabian horses with a fanatic's zeal. He is said not only to have spent 4.5 million pounds gold on them, but also not to have shied from theft, extortion, and murder to possess valuable asil horses. The Wahabbi lost over two hundred of the most noble horses from Emir *Abdullah's* stud in 1813 as tribute after losing their war.

"When Ibrahim (Mohammed's eldest son) captured the Wahabbi's last stronghold in the

Nejd, the finest and largest group of Bedouin horses ever said to exist in Arabia fell into his possession." (J. Forbis)

This peace settlement may not even seem worth mentioning to us, being accustomed to the astronomical reparation statistics of the Second World War. But in Arabia, ownership of purebred horses outweighs the ownership of anything else. It is unequalled, and the true value of purebred horses can only be compared to the great artworks of Western civilization, the loss of which effects the entire nation. Every single one of these precious animals was as irreplaceable as a work by Phideas, or a painting by Raffael. (*C. Raswan*)

It is remarkable that Mohammed Ali had gathered over eleven hundred of the most outstanding horses to his luxurious stables. *"When finally he became insane, the grooms, who had always been trembling for their lives, took their revenge on the guiltless creatures by neglecting and starving them in their marble stables. Sometimes the rotting carcasses lay there for days. Dying horses stumbled about the place. Unspeakable horror surrounded the royal stables." (C. Raswan)*

Ibrahim Pasha secured for himself some of these purebred horses, but there were also great problems at his stud. Colonel *Howard Vyse* reported in 1840 after visiting the Ibrahim Pasha stud that he found the approximately two hundred and fifty broodmares there in a far more critical state than the horses at the Mohammed Ali stud at Schoubra. Help for Schrouba, although not very significant, came from *Abbas Pasha*, Mohammed Ali's grandson, who saved some of the horses by bribing the staff.

He later led the Arabian breed of horse to a new world repute. He had, however, seen the results of Egyptian stable management, so he employd excellent Arabian Bedouin staff. They managed the stud according to the strict Bedouin rules!

Abbas Pasha was probably the most outstanding personality ever to put himself at the service of the asil treasures, which he did skillfully and with great expertise. Even today, the legendary Abbas Pasha's manuscript is a wellspring of the most important information on breeding asil Arabians. Through the deserving and expert work of Mrs. *Judith Forbis,* wellknown author and famous breeder an English translation will soon be available.

Abbas Pasha was succeeded by his son, *El Hami Pasha,* who was not interested in horse breeding. So, after Abbas Pasha's death and only three years after his son's taking office, this wonderful stud came to an end. The stock was scattered to the winds. Hundreds of horses were sold abroad, especially to Europe. Some of the stock was bought by Ali Pasha Sherif, and in 1873 his stud reached its zenith with almost four hundred horses.

However, the next disaster was close at hand. In 1880, an epidemic broke out which caused the complet loss of many strains. Some ten years later, this magnificent stud was near the point of dissolution. Its achievements are now only a landmark of that part of Arabian history. (*Greeley*)

Two Europeans, *Willaim Scaven Blunt* and *Lady Anne Blunt*, saw the wonderful horses owned by Ali Pasha Sherif at that time. The Blunts found them so admirable that they secured some of them for themselves. They brought them to Europe and founded a famous stud which, as we know, was later to a great extent degraded by the introduction of SKOWRONEK blood. (Especially those lines which returned home from England to Egypt, were preserved asil).

Lady Anne hoped for success by founding a stud in Egypt with Sheikh Obeyed. In spite of their attention to their horses' welfare, the Sheikh Obeyed stud was not an unlimited success. Because of the heat, the insects, and, obove all, the grooms' carelessess and neglect of the horses while the Blunts were away in England, they decided to limit the stock kept there. The bulk of the stock was transferred to Crabbet Park. (*Greeley*)

It hardly seems credible that, at the start of the 20th century, the Royal Agricultural Society (R.A.S.) had to begin with such a deplorably poor number of broodmares. As already

The famous mare of El Zahraa
MONIET EL NEFOUS
(Shaloul – Wanisa)

mentioned, in the beginning there were sixteen foundation mares, as well as twenty horses brought back by the Blunts and the donations made in the 20's and 30's.

Unfortunately, the influence of the royal, and later, the national stud known today as El Zahraa, did not always lead to steady progress.

After a Golden Age in the 20's and 30's under the fortunate direction of *Prince Mohammed Ali* with horses like FADL (a Kuhaylan-Jellabi, a famous strain that today is very rare) or MAHROUSSA, there was another backslide in the late 40's. Finally, in 1949, the legendary Austrian-Hungarian General *von Pettko-Szandter* was acquired to direct the stud. What did the stud look like when he first came to see it?

"When General Szandter assumed control of the stud farm, he selected only 25% of the broodmares. Of the premier stallions, he kept only one. His reasons were their physical faults, untypiness, or incomplete pedigrees." (Laszlo Montosory)

"The stallions which were present in 1949, when I took over management of the El Zahraa stud farm, were mostly old, partly very old. Many had hereditary faults and were mostly unfit for the standard which ought to be set for stallions standing at stud to raise the general level of horse breeding in Egypt. During the past six years I have been able to replace about 50% of this faulty stock and to replace it with younger, newer, better stallions of known origin." (v. Pettko-Szandter)

Even to the present day, Egypt has drawn on the accomplishments of Pettko-Szandter.

During the Nasser revolution there was again danger of the whole achievement falling into ruin, but favorable circumstances prevented disaster, thanks especially to the help of *H.E. Sayed Marei.*

Only ten years ago conditions at El Zahraa were poor again. The broodmare herd was consistently underfed. The abortion rate and the mortality rate – especially for foals – was far beyond that of any other state stud in the world. Since then, the expert leadership of *Dr. Ibrahim Zaghoul* has restored the lacking care.

Those who would evaluate these horses' quality must picture for themselves these highs and lows of the asil Arabian breed. If, in spite of all this, the Egyptian Arabian still includes some very fine specimens, *how very prepotent must those few foundation mares have been? What sort of horses must they have been, those thousands of purebred desert Arabians, especially those from the Nejd? A very few of them were able to found such brilliant breeds throughout the world! (Olms)*

Many of the asil horses in Europe and the USA trace partly or wholly back to horses descended from those used in Egypt.

GASSIR (Kheir – Badia)
The energetic and stocky stallion was a
good mover and possessed solid bones and
four dark hooves

Senior stallion at El Zahraa
EL SARIA (Shaloul – Zareefa) showed a
model stallion expression and excetted by
his wonderful bay coat, deep black legs
and four dark hooves

Taking all these factors into account, especially the renewed interest in the Arabic countries, one should remember when referring to 'straight' Egyptians:

These horses are asil Arabians, descendants of the purebred horses of Arabian Deserta, especially of the Nejd. To truly be consistent with regional breeders of Arabian horses who use the term 'straight' to mean 'of their country', one really ought to say 'straight Arabian'!

No less a man than the outstanding *C. G. von Wrangel* – which equine expert could compare with him today? – said: *"Nobody who knows the actual conditions will ever speak of the 'real' Egyptian, Syrian, or Turkish Arabian horse. In the true sense of the word, 'real Arabians' are only those bred in the former Wahabbite kingom, the Nejd, and their direct offspring."*

Those knowledgeable in the subject, as well as the influential Arab potentates – especially the princes and sheikhs of Saudi Arabia – do not appreciate having their age-old breed referred to as Egyptian horses. An Arab values primarily descent from the Arabian peninsula, especially from the Nejd. The more direct the connection to the home breeding grounds, the better. Thus, for example, descent from the TURFA line is particularly admired (not for nothing has a Turfa Club been established). TURFA (strain: Obeyan Al Hamrah) was a royal gift from the King of Saudi Arabia, *Abdul Aziz* to the English court.

This valuable blood line is barred from the Pyramid Society by geographical frontiers. It is equally incomprehensible that not even El Zahraa or other Egyptian studs are allowed to use asil Arabians from the Arabia Deserta, the true original Arabians, for the vital outcrosses, without their products losing their status as Straight Egyptians. In view of the fact that individual breeders tend to erect tight walls around the bloodlines they themselves happen to have in their stables, stressing show qualities without regard to any performance criteria, the thowback for the breed is pre-programmed. Asil Club and Al Khamsa know about the high value of the original Arabian and the selection with a view to athletic horses.

In the Preface of "Asil Arabians vol. II", State Equerry Dr. G. Wenzler says: *"The Asil Club aims to preserve the asil Arabian with great care, in order to create a reserve of blood for future breeding programs, particularly in view of the danger of the Eastern sources of blood progressively drying up....The members confirm that the Arabian is primarily an outstanding general utility horse for sport and recreation, the true Arabian being a high-performance horse which will degenerate if not used in that manner. Therefore, it must be subjected to continuous performance tests and constant, strict selection. The objective is to strive for the*

Arabian's original image, and to preserve the lean, noble type and its innate capacity for high performance, as well as its undemanding nature."

Clearly, no breeder should anxiously hoard his treasures, and the best bloodlines are just good enough. But the horses should not be wrapped in cotton and set up on a smooth lawn. Just let us recall FADL (IBN RABDAN x MAHROUSSA).

FADL was the son of one of the most striking, handsome stallions and one of the most beautiful mares in Prince Mohammed Ali's stud. His later owner, Babson, dared to use him not only in polo, but also in the strenuous distance rides in the USA, also very successfully. He was a winner several times over, and handsome as well.

Breeding in-strain as described in Chapter III is hardly to be found any more. Therefore, all the more effort must be made to preserve the asil Arabian, so that we shall not lose its pure blood, with its resistance against inbreeding, its genetic consistency, its prepotence, and its noble temperament. The degree to which this prepotency can improve the European and American domestic Arabian especially, has been seen in part in the Polish Arabian breeding use of asil stallions. Today, we may admire the splendid results of introducing NAZEER sons and grandsons into the American and European studs which breed Arabians.

Purebred Arabian breeders in Europe would be well-advised to restore something of the original desert type to their stud-bred lines by consistant breeding to eliminate the influence of foreign blood (Uppenhorn, 1977).

A vehement backlash toward returning to the traditional ways is occurring in the Arabic countries.

A decree by *King Chalid Ben Abdulaziz* stated that only asil Arabian horses may be imported. And when an Arab says asil, he means asil. Why would it even occur to the Prince, who imported several Arab horses to Saudi Arabia, that a purebred was not a purebred at all? Why would he suspect in the least that, in some cases, a but cursory inspection would reveal to experts many ancestors of foreign or unknown blood? I dare not imagine the harsh curses uttered in the flowery Arabic language by the person concerned."

CHAPTER X

RESULTS OF BREEDING WITH ARABIAN BLOOD

In this chapter, we will investigate the potential offered by cross-breeding with Arabian blood, as shown in three examples. The models selected use the breeding results among three world-famous breeds: the Orlov Trotter, the English Thoroughbred, and the French Anglo-Arab – a trotter, a racehorse, and an event horse. This demonstrates the wide-ranging possibilities offered by the Arabian. It will be especially emphasized that selection according to performance was of decisive importance in developing each of these three breeds. The bases for developing a new breed are:

1. Increasing the genetic variation by crossbreeding.
2. Strict selection for the desired characteristics.
3. Consolidation of characteristics by inbreeding.

The Orlov Trotter's history is a text-book example.

The Orlov Trotter

Count Alexei Grigoriewitch Orlov-Tschesmenskii was a favorite of Czarina Catherine the Great, who reigned from 1762 to 1796. In 1770, however, Count Orlov fell into disgrace, and he thereafter devoted his energies to breeding fast trotting horses – a venture of lasting success, as we now know. He had in mind a tough horse that could swiftly take a coach or sleigh long distances in Russian terrain and climate. It was also to be refined, and show good trotting action. After a few unsuccessful attempts, he remembered the Arabian's toughness and enormous endurance. In 1775, he bought a number of Arabians from Morea, Greece, to his Ostrovo Stud near Moscow. The desert Arabian, SMETANKA, was among these, a 15.3 hh grey stallion with a very good trot. Bred to a Danish mare, he produced the stallion, POLKA I, foaled in 1778. As *Nissen* (1964) described her, the Danish mare was tall, long, and strongly built, and she probably had a good deal of Oriental blood herself.

Winner of the German Derby:
OROFINO, Zoppenbroich Stud.
Photograph: H. Menzendorf

The half-Arabian POLKA I was not what Count Orlov had been aiming for at all. He had inherited all of his desert Arabian father's good points, but lacked freedom of shoulder movement. So, Orlov bred POLKA I with a Dutch trotting mare with tremendous shoulder freedom. This mare also carried a good deal of Oriental blood. In 1784, this cross produced the grey stallion, BARS I. BARS I stood at the Chrenovoi Stud for 17 years, and became the foundation sire for all Orlov Trotters. Because of his mixed breeding, however, he produced inconsistently.

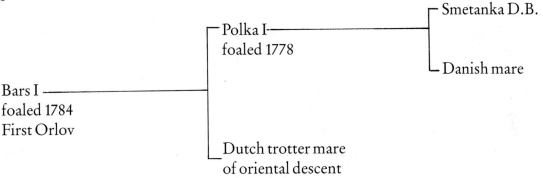

Aside from BARS I, Count Orlov had a number of POLKA I get, including a few mares, i.e., half-sisters to BARS I. Crossing BARS I with these half-sisters produced especially excellent offspring. By inbreeding to POLKA I, he could retain the stallion's good points, while the Dutch trotting mare's shoulder freedom was also passed to the next generation through BARS I. In this manner, Count Orlov bred the very good stallions POCHWAL-NIJ BARISCH-BOLSCHOI, and URSAN I.

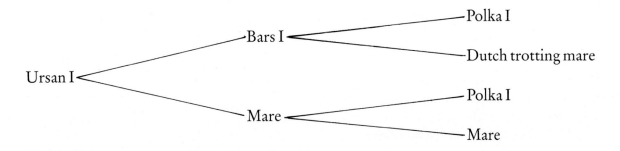

The mares used were, among others, top-grade Ukrainians and Mecklenburgers as well as English Thoroughbreds (*Saurel*, 1968).

All horses were subjected to strict selection by performance, before being used as breeding stock. The shortest distance they were tested over was about a quarter mile (426.7 meters), the record time for which was in the neighbourhood of about 30 seconds, the longest distance was 20 Worst (about 20 miles).

After Count Orlov's death in 1809, his serf, Schischkin, carried on breeding Orlov Trotters. He first tried to consolidate the breed by inbreeding. This led to a loss of size unsuitable for a coach horse.

To restore size, Schischkin fell back to the Dutch trotting mares. From one of these mares he produced the stallion, LJUBESNEC III, in 1835. This stallion sired the influential stallion, WARWAR I, who in turn sired 19 breeding stallions for the Orlov Trotter Stud in Chrenovoi.

It is interesting to see how, for the Orlov Trotter, the influence of one single stallion during the foundation period could be maintained for so many generations through inbreeding and selection. This example clearly shows how consistant inbreeding to only a few horses at the beginning of a pedigree maintains the original inheritance even after many generations. The same can be concluded from the results of Polish Arabian breeding.

The English Thoroughbred

The Thoroughbred (or English Thoroughbred) has a history dating from the pre-Roman era. In 55 B.C., Julius Ceasar mentioned the English cavalry in *De Bello Gallico*. This cavalry rode small, tough, native horses, which were probably the ancestors of or related to the modern Exmoor pony (*Nissen*, 1964).

Especially in the coastal regions, some of them had Oriental traits. The Roman legions had brought horses from the East with them to Belgium and northern France, and from there over the Channel to England.

At the time of the occupation of Yorkshire by the Roman troops under Septimus Severus (206–210 A.D.), the first horse races were held at Weatherby in York. This sporting event was enthusiastically welcomed by the English populus (*Tesio*, 1965). Others say that the first horse races were held during the prehistoric period, thinking perhaps of Stonehenge (*Nissen*, 1964). This is conjecture, however.

In the 10th century, Eastern blood again reached English shores. Hugo Capet (987-996) sent King Athelstan a few "Moorish" (north African) horses when Capet was wooing the King's sister's hand.

William the Conqueror (reigned 1066–1087) also imported "Moorish" horses, but the first desert Arabian reached England under Henry I (reigned 1100–1135).

In 1099, the First Crusade was crowned with the conquest of Jerusalem. Over the next century, five Crusades were undertaken, from which many knights brought back Eastern horses. The first documented importation of Eastern horses was in 1533, though: a letter from Baltasare Castiglione, ambassador to King Henry VIII, to his prince, Frederico II, Duke of Mantua. In this letter, the ambassador requests Frederico II to present the English king with a few broodmares from his Eastern racehorse stud in Mantua. The request was granted, and a letter from Henry VIII thanking him for "illo equorum genera" has been preserved. During the same period, Catherine of Savoy, daughter of the Spanish King Philipp II also sent the English king a few Eastern broodmares from her famous racehorse stud in Turin. This document is still in the archives in Turin (*Tesio*, 1965).

In Italy at this time, horse races were very much in fashion. Even racing strategies had been thought up. Baltasare Castiglione wrote a letter to his jockey advising him not to push the horse right after the start, but rather to make his best move just shortly before the finish.

Forty years later, England again turned to Italy for help. The royal stables were in poor condition. Count Leicester, Master of the Horse under Queen Elizabeth I, turned to the famous Italian racehorse authority, Signore Prospero d'Osma for advice on restoring the royal stables to their former brilliance. Don Prospero answered in a hand-written letter elegantly bound in leather, dated 1576. In 1917, this letter was publicly sold in London for 115 pounds. The buyer was the American, Mr. Alfred Maclay.

According to Tesio, the actual history of the English Thoroughbred begins with this letter in 1576. This manuscript records the names of all broodmares then in the English Royal Stud, and the stallions to which they were bred. Names such as SAVOY and BRILLADORO indicate that they were direct offspring of Eastern broodmares from Italy.

Prospero wrote, among other things, that it would be inadvisable to cross two breeds of horses, since this inevitably leads to breeding among half-breds. In fact, this document shows that the broodmares such as SAVOY, BRILLADORO, and others, were bred exclusively to stallions from the East.

From this, *Tesio* (1965) concluded that contemporary authors were mistaken in their opinion that the English Thoroughbred was the product of crossing native English mares with Eastern blood. Their conclusion was incorrect. The great, classic winners had almost exclusively Eastern ancestors.

MENHA (Mohawed – Nagwa), Reserve Champion Mare, Asil Cup International 1986, dam of HAMASA EL FAGR, National Supreme Champion of South Africa. This outstanding mare shows why Arabians have so successfully been used in breeding trotters.
Bred by El Zahraa, Cairo
Owned by Olms Arabians Hamasa Stud

This claim by the famous racehorse authority, Frederico Tesio, deviates here from the popular conception, but his ideas seem better defendable to me. During the time of Elizabeth I, as writings testify, purely bred racehorses were used almost exclusively.

In Chapter VIII, we saw how fast a purebred Arabian is. It can hardly be assumed that these swift horses were bred to native horses, since the get would have had no chance against the purebred horses from the Near East on the track.

During the period between King James I (reigned 1603-1625) and George I's ascent to the throne in 1714, 170 more Eastern horses were imported. This, too, made the use of domestic blood highly unlikely, as these imports would have been far too tough competition for the domestic horses.

After this period, it is fairly certain that no domestic breed of horse was used, since John Cheney distributed his first racing calendar in 1727. This racing calendar appeared annually in England initially, and later in other countries as well. Much information about the individual racehorses was given in these calendars.

No account of the English Thoroughbred would be complete without mentioning the most famous foundation sires.

The BYERLY TURK, foaled in 1680, was captured from the Turks near Vienna by Captain Byerly. Through his son, JIGG, he became the foundation sire to the Herod line.

The DARLEY ARABIAN, a Mu'niqi-Hadruj from the Anazeh Bedouins, was bought in Aleppo by the English ambassador, Mr. Darley, for his brother. The stallion's son, THE FLYING CHILDERS, foaled in 1715, 14.3 hh., was a mail coach horse in Hull, but later won 5 races and was considered the fastest horse of his time.

The GODOLPHIN ARABIAN must have been a Barb, with a roman nose. He is reported to have been a gift from the Bey of Tunis to the King of France. In 1728, he came to England. He sired the famous racehorse, LATH, and was grandsire to MATCHEM (1748) and ECLIPSE (1764). All modern Thoroughbreds can be traced back to these three stallions.

Part I of Mr. Weatherby's studbook appeared in 1793, in which about 100 mares and 100 stallions are entered. Uppenhorn gives a very meaningful definition of the term "Thoroughbred:" English Thoroughbreds are those horses which Messrs. Weatherby have said are English Thoroughbreds. Initially this was a closed studbook, i.e., all newly entered horses had to trace to ancestors already included in Messrs. Weatherby's *General Stud Book*. After 1901, it was opened to horses which had been purely bred for 8 or 9 generations within a period of 100 years, and which had successful racehorses as near relatives.

As already mentioned, the *General Stud Book* of 1793 included about 100 mares and as many stallions. These were, as Tesio explains, of practically exclusive Eastern breeding. Only a few were of unknown origins, which does not necessarily mean that they were not of Eastern blood as well.

Over the years, though, most lines died out, so the modern English Thoroughbreds are descendants of the 3 foundation sires mentioned and only 42 of the approximately 100 mares appearing in the *General Stud Book*, Part I, 1793.

True, some stallions besides those three do live on through the female lines, such as the AL-COCK ARABIAN, but that plays little role, given the overall dominant inbreeding to those three.

If, for simplicity's sake, we assume an average of ten years between 2 generations, there are about 18 generations between 1793 and today. A horse has 2 parents, 4 grandparents, 8 great-grandparents, and 16 great-great-grandparents – bringing us to the 4th generation. By the 18th generation, the number of ancestors rises to about a quarter of a million. But there were only about 200 horses registered in 1793, and, of these, more than half are not present in modern Thoroughbred pedigrees. We may then conclude that each of these ancestors must appear 2500 times in the modern English Thoroughbred's pedigree: During these 18 generations, then, these ancestors of 1793 were inbred 2500 times; that was possible only on the basis of tremendously strict selection at the racetrack.

Our purebred Arabian breeding, too, shows heavy inbreeding. For an example, I have chosen a lovely stallion bred in England, foaled in 1965 and exported to Holland. I have investigated his parentage up to and including the 9th generation. By the 9th generation, which includes 512 ancestors, the desert Arabian, MESAOUD, or his parents, appear 34 times. Such inbreeding tends to consolidate desireable qualities, but lacking selection for performance and appearance, it must eventually go awry.

For the 3rd example of successful breeding and skillful use of Arabian blood, I have chosen the French Anglo-Arab. This breed has developed into a very good event horse in France.

The French Anglo-Arab

Actually, it is a bit misleading. In Holland, there is also a studbook for Anglo-Arabs – two, in fact: one for Anglo-Arab purebreds, and one for Anglo-Arab half-breds. We are not, correctly speaking, referring to one breed. It is, quite simply, a cross-breed. A comparable

Lt. Col. de Beauregard, Cadre Noir,
Saumur, riding an Anglo-Arabian.
Photograph: R. Hebel

situation is found in England, Germany, and other countries. But in France the case is entirely different. The French have in fact created a new breed of horse over the last century and a half. The breed is called the Anglo-Arabian. It is a breed because the genetic characteristics are fixed by consistant breeding of Anglo-Arab to Anglo-Arab, and by strict selection according to performance. By 1942, 2 separate registries were kept for Anglo-Arabs – the purebred and the half-bred. After 1942, these registries were combined and one spoke correctly only of Anglo-Arabs. No differentiation was made between the pure- and the half-bred horses.

When a Frenchman speaks with justifiable pride of his Anglo-Arab as a "pur sang Francais," it is equaivalent to the term "German purebred" as regards a Trakhener of purely German Trakhener blood.

The French Anglo-Arab breed is comprised of three components:

1) Native French mares.
2) Purebred Arabians.
3) English Thoroughbreds.

The native mares were Tarbaiser and Limousine horses – once-famed breeds from south-western France. Their breeding region had once been occupied by the Saracens. In 712, the French leader, Charlemange, defeated the Moor's army at Poitiers and pushed the rest of them back over the Pyranees. Many Arabian horses thus fell into the victors' hands. They included many stallions, so they greatly influenced the French stock. The Tarbaisers and Limousines trace back to this influence, to which was due their great reputation in the French Army. They were famous for their endurance and nobility. The French Limousines were so prized at Louis XIV's court that, in 1751, the breeding region around Chateau de Pompadour was royally decreed to be Haras Royal – a royal stud for Limousine horses.

This stud was dispersed during the French Revolution. The palace was partially destroyed. In the following Napoleanic Wars, the French stock of horses was reduced sharply both in quantity and quality. The state was forced to take measures, if they were to have a battle-ready cavalry in the future. In 1833, Pompadour was restored in all its glory. It was once again a state stud, but now had the special task of providing southwestern France with Eastern stallions.

Since the breeding program intended to cull by performance, a racetrack was built at Pompadour. Perhaps this explains why English Thoroughbreds instead of Arabians were used to improve the Limousines. In any case, the French breeding directors began the experiment with the English Thoroughbred. The results were disappointing, however. It was left up to the breeding genius, Gayot, to repeat the experiment, but this time with resounding success. He had in mind a horse for use in the cavalry: a horse with the English Thoroughbred's speed, the Arabian's toughness, and the Limousine's size; a horse which could bear great hardships without sacrificing too much in the way of performance. With exceptional expertise, Gayot himself sought out his breeding stock. After few attempts, it was found that the best method of breeding the Arabian's and the English Thoroughbred's advantages into the Limousine was alternating breeding. The get of a Limousine and an Arabian was bred to an English Thoroughbred, and that get was in turn bred to an Arabian. In the 20th Century,

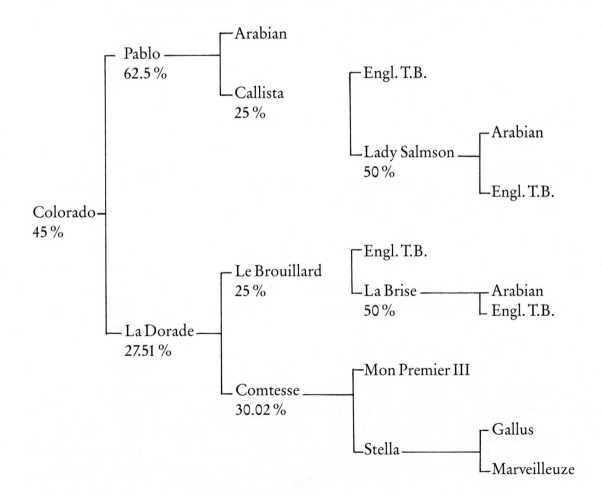

we frequently still find this pattern in French Anglo-Arabs' pedigrees, although Anglo-Arabs are also bred to Anglo-Arabs. A good example is the pedigree of the Anglo-Arab stallion, COLORADO, foaled in 1966 (with 45 % Arabian blood).

In the above pedigree, Anglo-Arabs stand under their own name, while Thoroughbreds and Arabians are marked as such. The percentage of Arabian blood is given under the Anglo-Arabs' names.

The female line – MARVEILLUEZE, STELLA, COMTESSE, LA DORADE, and COLORADO – record the results of breeding Anglo-Arab to Anglo-Arab. The stallions – LE BROUILLARD and PABLO – on the other hand – are the results of the alternating breeding method. This prevents the dominance of one or the other purebred breed. Too much Arabian blood could possibly lead to smaller get. There was an effort to breed faster horses for the racetrack by using more English Thoroughbreds, but it proved to lead to a loss of hardiness unfavorable to the Army. A minimum of 25 % Arabian blood was required for the Anglo-Arab. To circumvent the attempt to succeed on the track by breeding in the highest possible percentage of English Thoroughbred blood, the Anglo-Arabs were run in 2 separate divisions. As many races were held for the 50–99 % Arabian blood category as for the 25–40 % Arabian blood group.

Until 1960, six special races were also run each year for purebred Arabians. Since then, however, the purebred Arabians have run against Anglo-Arabs, so that that category now includes horses with 50–100 % Arabian blood.

The French Anglo-Arab is bred chiefly for performance. The government very much promotes this, and makes high performance stallions available. In Pompadour, the director, M. Pechdo, proudly exhibited these horses, along with the English Thoroughbreds, GREYHOUND (MOURNE x MIGRALIE) and WILD HUN (WILD RISK x HUNOLINE) – true kings of the racetrack who together earned over a million. GREYHOUND won the "Le Grand Steeple de Deauville," while WILD HUN had 14 wins and was in the money nineteen times.

Most Arabian stallions were imported to France from the French State Studs in Tunisia and Algeria. Many desert Arabians and some Egyptian stallions such as the famous IBN FAYDA, a full brother of IBN RABDAN, were also stood at stud. The Arabians used at stud must first have proven themselves on the track. So it was that OUROUR, grandsire of the stallion, JAZOUR, which I imported to Holland from France, had five wins and eighteen placings at the track. The genetic prepotency of the Arabian stallion, DENOUSTE, was remarkable. His 10 sons and grandsons produced 838 registered offspring in all.

Of these get, 271 had one or more wins at the great Concours Hippiques! The highest percentage of first place winners was supplied by ABEL's son, SEDUCTAUR (Anglo-Arab with 72.26% Arabian blood): of his 296 sons and daughters, 118 won a Concours Hippiques – almost 40%. ABEL, himself, an Arabian, won 3 races and placed 4 times (*U.N.I.C.*, 1971). But not only the State serves the Anglo-Arabs' interests. Much initiative is shown in the private sector, above all among the numerous regional breeding associations. They try to buy successful retiring racehorses, thereby preventing the loss of precious breeding stock, expensive though the horses may be.

Arabian Blood and Height at the Withers

Many are afraid to breed our sport horses to Arabians. One of the arguements given sounds rather convincing, but has been sufficiently refuted by the results of the French Anglo-Arab program. I am referring to the claim that the introduction of Arabian blood necessarily causes a loss of size. I have already addressed this in an article published in 1970 in connection with the public sale at Poitiers. The 48 Anglo-Arabs offered at auction there presented living proof of the possibility of maintaining height while raising that percentage of Arabian blood. Within that group, that percentage ranged from the required minimum of 25 % up 73.33 % in the chestnut mare, CODANA, by the Anglo-Arab, COQ DE BRUYERE, and out of the Anglo-Arab, BARBANE.

On an average, the Anglo-Arabs entered at Poitiers in 1970 had 41 % Arabian blood, and stood an average of 15.3 hh. From this group, we examined 10 horses with the least percentage of Arabian blood. This varied from 25 % to 31 %, averaging 27.5 %. This group's height ranged from 15.1 hh to 16.2 hh, with a mean of 15.3 hh.

The ten horses with the highest percentage of Arabian blood carried 50–73 % Arabian blood, or an average of 56.2 %. If crossing with Arabians does result in a smaller get, this latter group of horses, which carried twice as much Arabian blood, should have been smaller than the first group. However, there was no trace of this, as their height ranged from 15.0½ to 16.2 hh, with a mean of 15.3½ hh.

Not long ago, I had the opportunity to observe the influence of Arabian blood on height in Anglo-Arabs in Pompadour, thanks to the kind assistance of M. *Pechdo*, director of the Pompadour Stud. Thirty-nine Anglo-Arab mares and 27 stallions were measured. These horses were categorized by percent of Arabian blood, one with 25–50 % Arabian blood, and one with more than 50 %:

Group I: Mares   av. 38 % Arabian blood
                       av. height 15.3
Group II: Mares   av. 56 % Arabian blood
                       av. height 15.2–½
Group III: Stallions   av. 39.7 % Arabian blood
                       av. height 16.0
Group IV: Stallions   av. 57.8 % Arabian blood
av. height 16.0

Arabian blood had hardly any effect on height.

But looking at the various individual get themselves, we can identify quite variable results: The Arabian stallion, GOSSE DE BEARN, for example, produced a son, CANDAR, standing 16.1½ hh, out of the English Thoroughbred, CANDY. But his full sister, CANIQUE, never came near 15.3. One of the most striking results came from the desert Arabian, SOAKNE (14.1 hh) and the English Thoroughbred mare, NINAS. The foal NUNKY matured to a huge mare, nearly 2.5 hands taller than her sire. Of course, exceptions such as CANDAR and NUNKY are rare, but it is the breeder's task to consolidate these uncommon but desireable characteristics by expert selection.

All in all, we can conclude that the French Anglo-Arab breeders were able to raise the percentage of Arabian blood in sport horses without sacrificing size. Breeding Arabian blood into sport horses does raise the question of whether it is best done by using an Arabian mare or an Arabian stallion.

To answer this question, consider the results of *Walton's* and *Hamond's* experiments in Cambridge (1938). They bred Shetland ponies to the tremdenous Shires, with the help of artifical insemination, of course. The results indicated that the foals' birth weight was hardly influenced by the sires' size:

Sire		Dam	Birth Weight
Shetland	x	Shetland	37.4 – 39.6 lbs.
Shire	x	Shetland	37.8 lbs.
Shetland	x	Shire	117.7 lbs.
Shire	x	Shire	149.6 – 169.4 lbs.

One may infer that a large stallion can be bred to a small mare without too much risk. The difference in size first became apparent as the foals matured. At the age of 3, there were substantial differences:

Sire		Dam	3 yr. Old Get
Shetland	x	Shetland	9.3–½ hh.
Shire	x	Shetland	11.3 hh.
Shire	x	Shire	16.1–½ hh.
Shetland	x	Shire	12.2–½ hh.

To maintain offspring size, therefore, it is better to breed a large mare to a small stallion than vice versa. However, this is no law of general validity. There are always exceptions. In 1966, the Anglo-Arab stallion, COQ DE BRUYERE (16.1 hh) at Pompadour, bred 3 mares whose foals matured to quite varying sizes:

Cinette (15.2 hh)   produced Cadix 15.3 hh
Crevette (16 hh)   produced Carlita 15.1½ hh
Crete Royale (15.3 hh) produced Castille 15.1½ hh

CARLITA as well as CASTILLE stayed smaller than either parent. Here, the larger stallion produced smaller get.

The Anglo-Arab stallion, LAON (16.1 hh), on the other hand, sired foals out of the Arabian mares, BASSALA (14.3 hh) and ABLETTA (14.3 hh) which, as 3 year olds, were 1 to 1.5 hands taller than their dams:

LAON (16.1 hh) x BASSALA (14.3 hh) produced Banderille (15.3 hh)
LAON (16.1 hh) x ABLETTE (14.3 hh) produced Amigo (15.3–½ hh)

The Anglo-Arab mare, ALMERIA (15.0–½ hh) was sired by the English Thoroughbred WILD HUN (16 hh), yet remained as small as her dam, the purebred Arabian mare ARBA-LETE (15.0–½ hh).

From these few examples it is clear how difficult it is to anticipate get's size. Only among very consistently-bred lines would there be any certainty.

TRANSLATOR'S NOTES

Not every language presents the typical horseman with quite the confusion over the terms 'Thoroughbred,' 'thoroughbred', 'purebred', and 'registered' that English does. Are Quarter Horses thoroughbreds if they are sired by a Thoroughbred? Can a Thoroughbred sire a registered, purebred Hanoverian? If Thoroughbreds are purebreds, is there such a thing as a purebred Standardbred? If a horse is registered, is it a purebred? Is it a Thoroughbred? The answer to all these questions is a firm "maybe". The problem arises from at least three circumstances: 1) it is rather common to use the words 'thoroughbred' and 'purebred' interchangeably for many species; 2) the British chose to call one of the foremost sporthorse breeds the ‚Thoroughbred' (with a capital 'T'); and, 3) Thoroughbreds are frequently used to improve other breeds, so an individual Thoroughbred might be approved by more than one registry, and therefore beget offspring registered in different studbooks.

Also, horses might be referred to by their country of birth or acquisition, which may co-incide with a specific breed name. Or, the area so designated may be rather indefinte or out-of-date. For example, ‚Arabia' frequently implies a larger but ill-defined area greater than just present-day Saudi Arabia. Furthermore, it can be much simpler forconversational purposes to describe a horse by the breed it mostly is or resembles, rather than go into a percentage breakdown of its ancestry. So some slackness regarding the use of these terms has become part of many horseman's habit.

In this translation, I have largely kept to the usage of 'purebred' when referring to horses of strictly one breed – although some antiquated quotes retain the earlier usage of 'thoroughbred' for the sake of verisimilitude. Refernces to the Thoroughbred as a distinct breed are always capitalized, and usually specify 'English Thoroughbred'.

With respect to the relationship between purity of blood and registration in a breed studbook, I refer the reader to Dr. Klynstra's comprehensive discussion of that matter in this book. Similarly, the occurrence of various spellings of the Arabic strain names is better explained in Chapter II.

It is a pleasure to bring to English-speaking horsemen this excellent book, whick seeks to clarify and bring factual evidence to bear on the many myths and misconceptions which surround the Arabian horse. By doing so, the breed's value to modern horsemen is made all the more solidly based.

While I have had the opportunity to work with even Olympic-level horses, it is in many ways a greater honor to have known and owned desert-bred horses. They are something very special.

I deeply regret that many horsemen, knowing Arabians only as 'showring ornaments', have gained the impression that Arabians are weak, flighty, and basically rather useless. For I have known many Arabians to be by far the kindest, most sensible, athletic, durable, and just plain ridable horses I've met on three continents. Those I have truly admired *always* turned out to have desert breeding.

Like the author, it is my hope that we horsemen will take a closer look at our resources, in terms of bloodlines and meaningful performance tests, and re-evaluate our breeding and use practices. For if a bloodline once admired enough to import from the other side of the world seems to be becoming less than it was, it is not the horses' fault, but our own.

I would like to acknowledge here Mr. Charles Craver of Hillview Farms and Mr. and Mrs. Horst Haenert of Pine Grove Farms, both in Illinois/USA, for their dedication to their remarkable desert-bred horses. I would also like to thank Mary Whelihan, Marybeth Schmitt, Christina Crisler, and Michael Kurasz for their help in preparing this translation.

I also commend you, the reader, for your love of excellence and beauty which prompts your interest in this book. May it serve you well in all your endeavors.

Virginia, 1988   Kathleen Schmitt

Bibliography

ABD-EL-KADER, EMIR, siehe: E. Daumas, Die Pferde der Sahara, 1853-54, Hildesheim, 1976.

AL KHAMSA ARABIANS. A Documentation of Al Khamsa Arabians and Their History. Inc. Rockfort, Ill. 1983.

ALY, PRINZ MOHAMMED, Egypt's Pure-bred Arabs. The History of he Arab Horse in Egypt. The Arab. Horse, 1936, siehe: The Inshass Studbook of Arabian Horse Breeding, Zutphen, 1973.

ALY, PRINZ MOHAMMED, Pure-bred Arab Horse and Their Breeding and Training, siehe: Conn, G. H., 1959, 201-210.

AMMON, K. W., Nachrichten von der Pferdezucht der Araber und den arabischen Pferden, Nürnberg, 1834 und Hildesheim 1972.

AMSCHLER, W., The oldest pedigree chart. Journal of Heridity, 26 (1935) 233.

ANTONIUS, O., Die Abstammung des Hauspferdes und des Hausesels. Die Naturwissenschaften, 1918, 13.

ANTONIUS, O., On the Geografical Distribution, in Former Times and To-day, of Recent Equidae. Proc. Zool. Soc. London, B 107 (1937) 557.

ASHOUB, ABDEL ALIM, History of the Royal Agricultural Society's Stud of Authentic Arabian Horses, Cairo, 1948.

ASIL ARABER/ASIL ARABIANS, Arabiens edle Pferde, The Noble Arabian Horses. Hildesheim, New York, 1977.

AWTOKRATOW, D. M., Variationen in der Reihe der Hals- und Brustwirbel beim Pferde, Anat. Anzeiger, 60 (1926) 529.

BAKELS, F., The Asil Arabian in the Light of New Genetic Knowledge. Hildesheim 1980.

BARAHMI, T., Untersuchungen über die Schädelkapazität der Equiden. Diss. Halle, 1926.

BILKE, E., Pferdepassion. Von Pferdezucht und Pferdeschönheit. Hildesheim 1976.

BLUNT, LADY A., A. Pilgrimage to Nejd. New York 1879 and Reprint Hildesheim 1983.

BLUNT, Sir WILFRED S., The forthcoming Arab race at New Market. Wallace's Monthly 1875/93. Siehe: Conn, G. H., 1959, 370.

BORDEN, SPENCER, The Arab Horse, 1906, Los Angeles 1961.

BRENNON, H. C., Eryhrocyte and Hemoglobin Studies in Thoroughbred Racing Horses. Journal Am. Vet. Med. Assoc. (1956) 343.

BROWN, W. R., The Horse of the Desert. New York, 1947, Hildesheim, 1977.

BROWN-EDWARDS, GLADYS, The Arabian-War horse to Show horse. The Arabian Horse Association of Southern California, 1969, 1973.

CHARD, T., An early horse skeleton. Journal of Heredity, 28 (1937) 317.

COLENBRANDER, Een Shetland-story. De Hoefslag, 44 (1969), 38.

COMFORT, A., A Life table for Arabian mares. Journ. Gerontolog., 17 (1962) 14.

CONN, GEORG, H., The Arabian Horse in Fact, Fantasy and Fiction. London, 1959.

DAMOISEAU, L., Hippologische Wanderung in Syrien und der Wüste. Leipzig 1842 und Hildesheim 1979.

DAUMAS, E., Die Pferde der Sahara. Berlin 1853-54, Hildesheim, New York 1976.

DAVENPORT, H., My Quest of the Arabian Horse. Reprint Boulder/Col. London 1911.

DRAHN, F., Halsrippen beim Rind und reduzierte Brustrippen beim Pferd in ihrer vergleichend-anatomischen Bedeutung. Zeitschr. Säugetierk. 1 (2) 1926, 121.

ETHERINGTON, M. G., Exmoor Ponies. Journal. Soc. Preserv. Fauna Empire New Ser., 53 (1946) 12.

FLADE, J. E., Das Araberpferd. Die neue Brehm Bücherei, Stuttgart, 1966.

FORBIS, J., The Classic Arabian Horse. New York 1976.

FREY, OTTO, Das arabische Pferd. 150 Jahre Weil-Marbach. Winterthur, 1968.

GRASHUIS, J., De voeding en verzorging van het paard. Uitgave Stichting C. L. O.-Controle en Instituut voor Moderne Veevoeding „De Schothorst", Hoogland.

GREELY, M., Arabian Exodus. London 1976.

GUTTMANN, U. und F. B. KLYNSTRA, The Lineage of the Polish Arabian Horses. Die Abstammung der polnischen Araber. Marbach, 1968.

HABERLAND, R., Die Bergpferde in den Waldkarpaten, Reiter Revue Int., 12 (1969) 992.

HAGEDORN, A. L., Animal Breeding. 5. Aufl. London, 1954.

HALTENORTH, TH., Pferde, Kosmos-Lexikon der Naturwissenschaften. Stuttgart, 1955.

HAMMER-PURGSTALL, J. FREIHERR VON, Das Pferd bei den Arabern. Vienna 1856 and Reprint Hildesheim 1981.

HANCAR, F., Das Pferd in praehistorischer und früher historischer Zeit. Wien-München, 1955.

HANSEN, M. F. und A. C. TODD, Preliminary Report on the Blood Picture of the Arabian Horse. Journal Am. Vet. Med. Assoc., 118 (1951) 26.

HEUSSER, H., Ueber die Blutausrüstung des Pferdes und ihre praktische Bedeutung. Schweizer Archiv für Tierheilkunde, 94 (1952) 463.

HISTORICAL ATLAS of the Moslim Peoples. Djambatan, Amsterdam.

HOOYER, D. A., Notes on some fossil mammals of the Netherlands. Arch. Mus. Teyler, 10 (1947) 33–51.

JONES, W. E. und R. BOGART, Genetics of the horse. Ann Harbor, Michigan. U. S. A., 1971.

THE AL KHAMSA DIRECTORY, hrsg. v. Al Khamsa Inc. o. O. 1976.

KHALIFA, DANNAH AL, The living treasures of Bahrain. Bahrain, 1971.

KIRSCH, K.-H., Blut – Adel – Leistung. Hildesheim 1983.

KORAN, DE, vertaling J. H. Kramers, 4. Aufl. Amsterdam, 1974.

KRETSCHMAR, M., Pferd und Reiter im Orient. Hildesheim 1980.

KLYNSTRA, F.B., Het Anglo-Arabische Ras, De Hoefslag, Jaarboek, 1969/70, 76.

---- Anglo-Arabes, Arabisch Bloed en Stokmaat, De Hoefslag, 1970, no. 17, 13.

---- Reinbloed en Volbloed Arabieren, De Hoefslag, 1970, no. 51, 7.

---- Reinbloedtheorie voor Arabische Paarden van Mohammed, De Hoefslag, 1971, no. 19, 12.

---- Arabische paardenrennen, De Hoefslag, 1972, no. 2, 16.

---- Een Cross over 160 kilometers, De Hoefslag, 1972, no. 16, 20.

---- Egyptische Indrukken, De Hoefslag, 1972, no. 29, 5.

---- Der Einfluß des Fremdblutes beim Araber, Sankt Georg, 1972, no. 12, 5.

---- Große Nüstern, schöne Köpfchen und zierliche Hufe, Reiter Revue Int., 1973, no. 7, 830.

---- Jordaanse Indrukken I–III, De Hoefslag, 1973, no. 34, 36; no. 35, 28; no. 36, 14.

---- Les courses de chevaux dans les pays arabes, in: R. Mauvy, Cheval de pur sang arabe, le cheval barbe. Paris 1976, 80–100.

---- Libanese Indrukken, De Hoefslag, 1974, no. 10, 7.

---- Woestijnarabieren en hun registratie, De Hoefslag, 1974, no. 12, A.P.S.-Nieuws, 35.

---- Het kruis van de Arabier, De Hoefslag, 1974, no. 16, A.P.S.-Nieuws, 33.

---- Hoe oud worden Arabische Volbloeds?, De Hoefslag, 1974, no. 47, A.P.S.-Nieuws.

LAWRENCE, J., The History and Delineation of the Horse. London 1809 and Reprint Hildesheim 1979.

LEHMANN, U., Die Fauna des Vogelherds bei Stetten ab Lontal (Württemberg). Neues Jahrb. Geol. u. Palaeontol., Abhandl. 99 (1), 1954.

LODEMANN, G., Das Pferdehaar. Tierzucht und Züchtungsbiol., Vol. IX (1927) 349.

LÖFFLER, E., Die österreichische Pferdeankaufsmission unter dem k.k. Obersten Ritter Rudolf von Brudermann. Troppau 1860 und Hildesheim 1978.

LUKOMSKI, B. v./J. BOROWIAK/F. v. DÜNKELBERG, Zum Arabischen Pferd. Stuttgart 1906, 1907, 1914 und Hildesheim 1979.

MAUVY, ROBERT, Le Cheval de pur sang arabe, le cheval barbe. Paris, 1964.

MAZAHERI, ALY, Zo leefden de Moslims, Hollandia, Baarn, 1969.

METTLER, L.E. und F.G. GREGG, Population genetics and evolution. London, 1969.

MUELLER, JOHN HENRY, Verrat in schwarzen Zelten. Zürich, 1977.

NIEBUHR, CARSTEN, Beschreibung von Arabien aus eigener Beobachtung, usw. Kopenhagen, 1972.

NISSEN, JASPER, Das Sportpferd. Stuttgart, 1964.

NURETTIN ARAL - E. SELAHATTIN: Der heutige Stand der Pferdezucht in Arabien, Züchtung: B. Tierzüchtung und Züchtungsbiologie Bd. 33, Heft 1, S. 13–38, Berlin, 1935.

OSBORN, H.F., Points of the skeleton of the Arab Horse. Bull. Amer. Nat. Hist. 5, 23 (1907) 259.

OLMS, W.G., Arabisches Reinblut, adé? Sankt Georg, no. 11, 1972.

---- Arabisches Reinblut, eine Fata Morgana? Sankt Georg, no. 1, 1973.

OLMS, W. G., Die Asil Araber – Dokumentation als Konzentrat überzeugender Argumente. Vortrag, gehalten vor dem Asil Club, Delingsdorf, 23. Juni 1984.

OLMS, W.G., Der Asil Club – Aufgaben, Ziele. Vortrag, gehalten vor dem Asil Club in Treis/Lda. am 31.5.1980.

OLMS, W.G., Al Khamsa or the Five Pillars of Arabian Breeding. El Asil – Character – Performance – Type – El Asil. Lecture held at the Al Khamsa, Inc. Meeting Aug. 27th, 1982, Rockford, I 11.

OPPENHEIM, M. v., Die Beduinen. Leipzig und Wiesbaden 1939 – 1968 und Reprint Hildesheim 1984.

PHILBY, H., Das geheimnisvolle Arabien. Leipzig 1925 und Reprint Hildesheim 1986.

PIDUCH, E., Arabian Horses of El Zahraa. Hildesheim 1982.

POZO LORA, R., Estimaciones biometricas en la rasa arabe des Espana. Arch. Zoot. Cordoba, 1956, zitiert nach Flade, 1966.

PULLING, FRED. B., Observations on Arabian Horses in the Near East. Journal American Veterinary Medical Association, 113 (1948), 130-133.

RASWAN, CARL R., The Arab and His Horse. 3. Aufl. Oakland, California, 1955.

---- Im Land der schwarzen Zelte. Berlin 1951, Hildesheim und New York, 1976.

---- The Raswan Index. Mexico, St. Barbara, 1957–1967.

---- Söhne der Wüste. Hildesheim und New York, 1977.

---- Trinker der Lüfte. Zürich, Stuttgart, Wien, 1942. Hildesheim und New York, 1977.

---- Tribal areas and migration lines of North Arabian bedouins. Geograph. Revue New York, 20 (1950) 494.

RASWAN, CARL R. und URSULA GUTTMANN, Arabische Pferde. Winterthur, 1965.

RASWAN, C.R. – H. SEYDEL, Der Araber und sein Pferd. Reprint Hildesheim 1981.

REFERENCE HANDBOOK OF STRAIGHT EGYPTIAN HORSES, Volume IV. Lexington/Kentucky o.J.

ROMIJN, C., The red blood picture of the horse. Tijdschrift Diergeneeskunde, 73 (1948) 333.

SÄNGER, OTTO, (Hrsg.) Araber-Stutbuch von Deutschland. Vollblutaraber, Bd. 1, Hildesheim, New York, 1974.

SAUREL, ETIENNE, Le Cheval Paris, 1968.

SCHIELE, ERIKA, Arabiens Pferde, Allahs liebste Kinder. München, Bern, Wien, 1972.

SEYDEL, HANS, Das arabische Vollblut (Kuhaylan). Studien über seine Eigenschaften und seine Beziehungen zur deutschen Pferdezucht. Wiss. Archiv Landw. 9 (1933) 50 – 87.

SLOB, A., Beschouwingen over de Tarpan. Lutra, 8. (1966), 1.

SIMPSON, G.G., Horses. New York, 1951, 1970.

SMYTHE, R.H., What makes o good horse. London, 1957.

SOLINSKI, S. G., Reiter, Reiten, Reiterei. Hildesheim 1983.

SUMMERHAYS, R.S., The Arabian Horse in Great Britain. London, 1967.

SUGANA, GABRIELE MANDEL, Mohammed. Amsterdam, 1970.

TESIO, FREDERICO, Rennpferde. Stuttgart, 1965.

TWEEDIE, W., The Arabian Horse. His country and people, Engeland 1894, Los Angeles, 1961.

U.N.I.C., Abrégé de la production de l'ANGLO-ARABE en France, l'Eperon, Numéro Special, Avril 1971.

UPPENBORN, W., Pferdezucht und Pferdehaltung, Offenbach, 1970.

UPTON, R.D., Gleanings from the Desert of Arabia. London 1881 and Reprint Hildesheim 1985.

VERTER, W., H. MIX und J. MULLER, Die Veränderungen der Zellwerte und einiger biochemischen Daten des Blutes bei Sportpferden im Schritt, Trab und Galopp. Medizinische Tierklinik und Inst. für Gerichtl. Tierheilkunde der Veterinärmed. Fakultät der Humboldt-Univ., Berlin, 29. Nov. 1965.

WALTON, A. und J. HAMMOND, The maternal effects on growth and conformation in Shire horse – Shetland pony crosses. Proc. Roy. Soc. B 125, 1938, 311–335.

STUDBOOKS:

Araber Stutbuch von Deutschland, Band I, Olms Hildesheim – New York, 1974.

Hamdan Stables. Stutbook of Arabian Horses, Vol. I, Cairo, 1969.

Hengst- und Stutenregister für Arabisches Vollblut. Marbach, 1967.

Het Arabisch Paardenstamboek Nederland Reg. A.

Stud-Book Français, Registre des Chevaux Arabes et Anglo-Arabes. Tome I–III.

The Arab Horse Stud Book. England, Vol. I–XI.

The Arabian Studbook. Publ. by the Arabian Horse Club of America, Washington, 1918.

The Blue Arabian Horse Catalog. J.L. Ott, Hindsdale, Vermond, U.S.A. 1961–1969.

The Egyptian Agricultural Society. Animal Breeding Section. El Zahraa Arab Horse Stud. The Arabian Stud Book Volume II–III. Cairo, 1966–1972.

The Inshass Studbook of Arabian Horse Breeding. Zutphen/Cairo, 1973.

The Royal Agricultural Society. Animal Breeding Section. History of the Royal Agricultural Society. Stud of Authentic Arabian Horses, Cairo, 1948.

Studbook of the Netherlands Arabian Horse Club The N.A.C., 1952.

Stutbuch Weil-Marbach, 1817–1971. Band II. Dr. G. Wenzler, Bamberg, 1972.